New   r8·01

Date Due

JUN 11 97	JAN 2	OCT 4 00	
JUN 27	8 13 98		
JUN 30 97	SEP 30 98		
JUL 2 '97	OCT 24 98		
JUL 0 8 97	NOV 20		
SEP 12 97	DEC 08 98		
9/27	DEC 2 97		
OCT 27 98	DEC 21 99		
DEC 9	AUG 16 00		

5/97

Jackson
   County
      Library
         Services

HEADQUARTERS
413 W. Main
Medford, Oregon 97501

6-98

THE WOMAN'S DAY BOOK OF

HOLIDAY
CRAFTS

THE WOMAN'S DAY BOOK OF

HOLIDAY CRAFTS

BY THE EDITORS OF

WOMAN'S DAY

PENGUIN STUDIO

Woman's Day Staff

EDITOR-IN-CHIEF: Jane Chesnutt
CRAFTS EDITOR: Eleanor Schrumm
WRITER/EDITOR: Nadia Hermos
CAPTIONS WRITER: Carol Minkow
COMPUTER ILLUSTRATOR: Jason Teig
ASSISTANTS: Tracy Costaldo, Cristina Pires Ferreira, Philene Rivera

Penguin Studio Staff

PUBLISHER: Michael Fragnito
PROJECT EDITOR: Sarah Scheffel
BOOK DESIGNER: Kathryn Parise
JACKET DESIGNER: Jaye Zimet
PRODUCTION: Alix MacGowan
PRODUCTION EDITOR: Bitite Vinklers
COPY EDITOR: Barbara Albright

PENGUIN STUDIO
Published by the Penguin Group
Penguin Books USA Inc., 375 Hudson Street, New York, New York 10014, U.S.A.
Penguin Books Ltd, 27 Wrights Lane, London W8 5TZ, England
Penguin Books Australia Ltd, Ringwood, Victoria, Australia
Penguin Books Canada Ltd, 10 Alcorn Avenue, Toronto, Ontario, Canada M4V 3B2
Penguin Books (N.Z.) Ltd, 182–190 Wairau Road, Auckland 10, New Zealand

Penguin Books Ltd, Registered Offices:
Harmondsworth, Middlesex, England

First published in 1996 by Viking Penguin,
a division of Penguin Books USA Inc.

10 9 8 7 6 5 4 3 2 1

CIP data available
ISBN 0-670-86882-5

Printed in the United States of America
Set in Caslon 540

CONTENTS

Valentine's Day 85

Easter 113

A Word from Woman's Day

In the last four or five years, we at *Woman's Day* have noticed a real boom in decorating for the holidays, and not just at Christmas. Across the country, people are decorating their porches for Halloween, their dinner tables at Easter, even their backyards for Fourth of July picnics. We love the trend. We think *any* occasion that brings family and friends together is worth commemorating with a homemade decoration or craft, but holidays seem an especially fitting time. You're making memories, after all, and there's something very special about seeing a handmade Christmas ornament year after year, or that stuffed bunny you sewed for a child's first Easter.

The other reason we're so thrilled with this decorating rage is that it confirms something we've known for a long time: America loves crafts. We get letters from readers all the time, often with photographs of a craft project they've done. Some have obviously been crafting for years, but equal numbers happily admit they've never made a craft in their lives. We tried to keep that in mind as we put together this book, and I think it shows. The book includes projects for every skill level and an incredible range of interests and tastes—something for everyone.

Crafts are a very important part of *Woman's Day,* and I've long been proud of the projects we feature. That said, I'm sometimes even more impressed at how creative our readers can be. We received one letter, for example, from a woman who had planned to make the Halloween witches on page 202. When Halloween came and went before she could get started, she adapted our pattern to make her own adorable little Thanksgiving pilgrims.

And then there's a reader who saw the felt snowmen on page 42. We'd featured them as simple, easy-to-make little Christmas ornaments, but she'd done us one better and made a snowman for each guest at her Christmas dinner. She embroidered the guest's name on the back and used the personalized snowmen as placecards for the table.

I can't tell you how wonderful it is to get letters and photographs from readers like these. Their joy at having made the project is infectious, and I'm always so happy we were able to inspire them with an irresistible idea.

I'm proud of this book, and I know you're going to fall in love with many of the projects. Each and every one is a wonderful memory waiting to be made.

Jane Chesnutt
Editor-in-Chief

CHRISTMAS

To make it merrier
and brighter

Folk Art Holiday Wall Hanging

A large wall hanging like this can set a holiday tone in a hallway, a family room, or a child's bedroom. Hang it behind the buffet table at a party. Once you've made one, you'll find the technique easy to use for other decorative hangings of your own design.

WHAT YOU'LL NEED

- 1 yard 72-inch-wide medium-tan felt
- 9 x 12-inch felt blocks: 9 red, 4 dark green, and 1 each light green, brown, black, gold, and light tan

Get right into the spirit of things with dancing reindeer, adorable teddies, and a forest of charming little trees. Our Folk Art Holiday Wall Hanging is easy to stitch up with patience, easier still to treasure for years to come.

- 1 skein of 6-strand embroidery floss to match each color of felt
- tan sewing thread
- embroidery needle
- 12 black ¼-inch-diameter flat buttons for eyes
- 18 assorted ⅜-inch flat red buttons for buttons and berries
- 57 assorted ⅜-inch to ¾-inch buttons for tree ornaments
- tracing paper
- graph paper
- 3 plastic rings and a dowel, curtain rod, or pushpins for hanging
- fabric shears and small, sharp scissors
- yardstick
- straight pins

HOW TO MAKE IT

1. Stitch the background: Mark a 35½ x 44½-inch rectangle on the tan felt with a yardstick and pencil. (To make sure the corners are square, the diagonal measurements from top to bottom corners should be equal.) Cut out the rectangle with the shears. Turn 1¾ inches on the long edges to the back, and pin. With tan thread, machine-stitch ¼ inch from the raw edge (1½ inches from the folded edge). Hem the short edges the same way. Iron the edges lightly from the back.

2. Trim the red blocks: Stack up the red rectangles. Check to make sure that the corners are perfect right angles as before or by matching the corners to a piece of typing or graph paper. Trim wavy edges to make all the rectangles exactly the same, but keep their full size.

3. Make the patterns: Enlarge the bear and reindeer patterns on page 6, making each square 1 inch (see How to Enlarge Patterns, page 220). Enlarge the tree, page 4, on a photocopier to 8 inches tall or copy it on graph paper following the dimensions given. Trace the full-size pattern for the star, page 4.

4. Cut the felt shapes: Trace each pattern

piece separately. Cut out the patterns and trace 3 of each piece onto colored felt. Cut the felt shapes.

5. Appliqué the figures: Pin the smaller pieces face up to larger ones, following the pattern. Separate matching colors of thread to use 3 strands in 18-inch lengths. Thread the needle and knot the end of the thread; hide the knot between layers when sewing. **Bears and reindeer:** Sew the edges of the small pieces to the figures with straight stitches about ⅜ inch apart. **Trees:** Center and sew the trunk and star to one of the red rectangles with straight stitches. Appliqué the branches with random straight stitches in the 2 green threads to mimic pine needles.

STAR

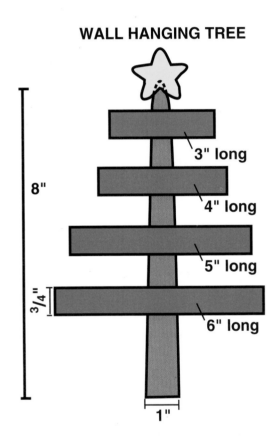

WALL HANGING TREE

8"

3" long

4" long

5" long

3/4"

6" long

1"

6. Sew on the buttons: Decorate the trees with buttons as ornaments. Sew the eyes on the bears and the reindeer, buttons on the bears' jacket and holly berries on the reindeer. Embroider stars with 6 strands of gold floss and straight stitches over the trees on bears' jackets.

7. Sew the figures to the blocks: Center each bear and reindeer on a piece of red felt. Check their placement by measuring from the edges to make them all the same. Then sew the edges in place with straight stitches as before.

8. Sew the blocks to the background: Pin the appliquéd blocks 1 inch apart on the tan background, placing the outer edges on the hem stitching and alternating the designs as in the photograph. Using 3 strands of tan floss, attach the edges of the blocks with a row of cross-stitches about ½ inch square and ½ inch apart. To cross-stitch, follow the diagram below, bringing thread up at A, down at B, up at C, down at D; carry it ½ inch across the back and repeat.

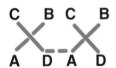

9. To hang the banner: Sew rings to the back 1 inch from the top edges at the corners and center. Insert a rod or dowel through the rings and hang the ends from hooks or brackets in the wall.

Teddy Bear and Reindeer Ornaments

Easy to display on wreaths, trees, and garlands or in a centerpiece, these felt ornaments could also be table favors at Christmas breakfast or dinner.

WHAT YOU'LL NEED (FOR TWO OF EACH)

- ¼ yard medium-tan felt
- 9 x 12-inch felt blocks or scraps in light tan, dark green, light green, red, brown, and black
- 1 skein of 6-strand embroidery floss to match each color
- embroidery needle
- eight 5mm black sequins and eight black seed beads for eyes
- fine needle for beads
- four ¼-inch red or white round or heart buttons for bear
- polyester fiberfill stuffing
- tracing paper
- sharp scissors
- wire cord or fish line for hanging

HOW TO MAKE THEM

1. Make the patterns: Enlarge the bear and reindeer patterns on page 6, making each square ¾ inch (see How to Enlarge Patterns, page 220). Then trace each pattern piece separately and cut them out (make the bear's body one piece to lie under the jacket). Cut the patterns from stiff paper or cardboard if you're making several ornaments.

2. Cut the felt: Trace the patterns for the ornament front onto appropriate color felt. Cut one of each piece, but two of each antler. Cut felt circles for holly berries.

3. Appliqué the fronts: Working from small to large, place the appropriate felt pieces over one another in the correct position. Cut an 18-inch length of thread matching the color of the smaller piece. Separate the strands of the thread and retwist them into pairs of two strands to use for sewing. Thread the needle and knot the end of the thread; hide the knot between the layers, then sew the pieces in place with straight stitches over the edges. Follow the pattern and photograph for placement. Do not attach the antlers. **Reindeer:** Sew the antlers together in pairs with stitches around the edges and set them aside. Sew running stitches along the center of the holly leaves with light-green floss, then attach the holly leaves and berries to the deer. **Bear:** After stitching the trees to the jacket, embroider the stars with six strands of gold floss. Sew two buttons to the jacket. **Eyes:** For each eye, place a sequin in the correct position and pull the thread up through the center of the sequin with the fine needle. Insert the

needle through a black bead, then continue sewing the bead through the sequin hole. Secure the thread in back.

4. Cut and stitch the backs: To make the backs, trace the completed ornament fronts onto the wrong side (rougher side) of tan felt, omitting the outer edge of the reindeer's holly. Cut out the backs. With the right sides out, pin the backs to the fronts. Insert the antlers at the top of the reindeer's head. Starting at the side of each bear or the center top of each reindeer, stitch over the edges with matching thread. Pause two inches before the end to insert the stuffing. Then finish stitching.

5. To hang the ornaments: Insert wire, cord, or fish line through the back and form a loop.

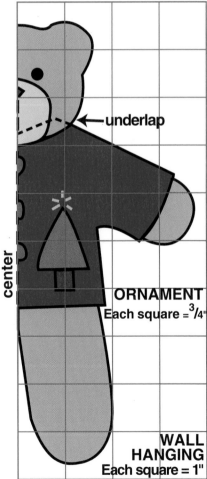

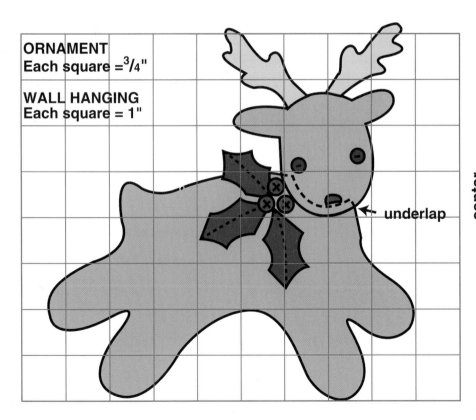

ORNAMENT
Each square = ³/₄"

WALL HANGING
Each square = 1"

← underlap

center

ORNAMENT
Each square = ³/₄"

WALL HANGING
Each square = 1"

> *S*anta's on a roll to add folk-art charm to your Christmas festivities and decorations.

Santa on Wheels

Any collector of old-fashioned toys, young or older, would be happy to receive this Santa as a gift.

SIZE

14 inches tall

WHAT YOU'LL NEED

- 24 inches of 1 x 10-inch pine or ¾-inch-thick plywood
- 6-inch dowel, ¼ inch in diameter
- primer or gesso
- acrylic paints in White, Brick Red, Butterscotch, Christmas Green, Light Periwinkle, and Azure Blue (FolkArt Colors by Plaid Enterprises)
- clear or satin water-based finish
- 2-inch-high wire tree or sprig of synthetic evergreen
- flat and round paintbrushes
- wood glue
- 1½-inch finishing nails
- medium and fine sandpaper
- masking tape
- drill
- saber saw
- tracing paper

HOW TO MAKE IT

1. Patterns: Enlarge the pattern, page 8 (see How to Enlarge Patterns, page 220). Trace a separate arm and wheel.

2. Cutting: Cut out the patterns and trace them onto wood. Also cut two 2⅜-inch lengths of dowel for the wheel axles. Sand the edges smooth. Place the cut-out pieces on scrap wood and drill ¼-inch-diameter holes through each wheel and the Santa for dowels. Slightly enlarge the holes in the Santa, either with a larger bit or by moving the drill. Drill a fine hole, as on pattern, down into the edge of one hand to hold the trunk of the artificial tree.

3. Painting: Transfer detail lines to both sides of the figure. Glue and nail an arm to each side. Prime and paint, following Making Wooden Cut-outs, page 221. Mix red, white, and a little blue to make flesh color for Santa's hands and face. As you paint the figure, make the colors flat or add dark and light areas to add shading where appropriate. When the paint is dry, "weather" the surface by rubbing it with sandpaper to let some white show through.

4. Finishing: Apply two coats of clear finish to the wooden pieces, letting each coat dry completely. Insert dowels through the holes in the Santa and glue a wheel to each end. Touch up the ends of the dowels with paint. Insert the wire trunk of the tree into the hole in Santa's hand.

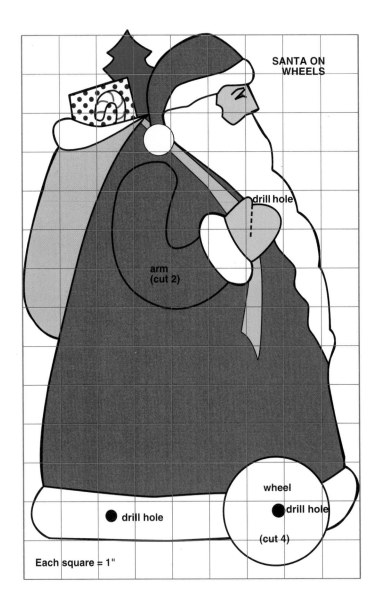

SANTA ON WHEELS

drill hole

arm (cut 2)

drill hole

wheel

drill hole

(cut 4)

Each square = 1"

Shimmering Angels

These angels are fairly detailed projects, so you might not want to make them by the dozen. A single one makes a special gift ornament, and three on a wreath would look wonderful.

SIZE

4½ x 6 inches

WHAT YOU'LL NEED (FOR 4)

- ¼ yard each white cotton knit and tissue lamé (or other fabric) for bodies
- 1 yard 3-inch-wide gold woven metallic ribbon or ¼ yard gold fabric for the wings
- 3 yards sportweight yarn for hair for each angel
- 1 yard ¼-inch-wide gold braided ribbon
- scraps of red and black embroidery thread for the eyes and mouths
- blush makeup
- polyester fiberfill stuffing
- fabric glue
- gold dimensional fabric paint in squeeze bottle (optional)
- graph paper
- drawing compass, can or small saucer to draw a 3¼-inch-diameter circle
- pencil or fabric marker

1. Make the patterns: Trace the patterns for the body, wing, hand and foot, below. On graph paper draw a 1¾-inch square for the arm pattern. Use the compass, or draw around a can or saucer to trace a 3½-inch circle for the head pattern.

2. Mark and cut the fabrics: Fold the fabrics in half, wrong side out, to cut patterns through two layers at once. If using lamé, see Working with Slippery Fabrics, page 222. Pin the body and arms to the lamé. Trace the outlines with pencil or fabric marker for the stitching line. Add a ¼-inch seam allowance all around the edges. Cut on the outer lines. Cut two more feet. **Head:** Cut the head from a single layer of knit. **Wings:** Cut the wings after assembling the body.

3. Paint the dots and lines (optional): Following the photograph, paint dots on the outside of the lamé gown front and the arms (tape the fabric down and be sure to practice painting on scrap fabric first; see box, page 11). Make a wavy line near the bottom of the gown. Let the paint dry flat overnight before stitching.

4. Stitch the pieces: Note: To sew all the seams, pin the pieces together in pairs, right sides together. Stitch the edges with a ¼-inch seam allowance, leaving an opening for turning. Clip into the seam allowance on the curves; turn the piece right side out.

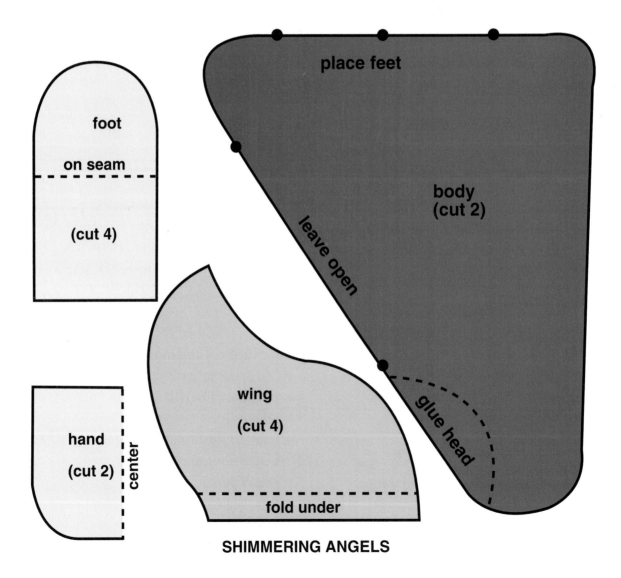

SHIMMERING ANGELS

Arms: Stitch a hand to each arm. Fold the arms in half lengthwise, right sides together. Stitch the edges, leaving the top open. Stuff to within a ½ inch of the top. Fold the shoulder diagonally down and tack it in place, reversing the fold on the second arm.

Feet: Stitch the feet together in pairs. Pin them to the right side of the body front between the dots, with the raw ends outward and the broken line on the seamline.

Body: Stitch the body back to the front, leaving an opening. Stuff the body. Sew the opening closed.

Head: Make a row of running stitches ¼ inch in from the edge of the circle. Gather the fabric along the thread. Stuff and shape the head so that the opening is at the back. Gather the opening tight; knot the thread and clip the ends.

5. Assembly: Following the photgraph, glue the head to the body. Glue the shoulder of one arm to the front and the other to the back, at angles that show both hands.

6. Wings: Cut the wings from gold material without adding a seam allowance. If the wing fabric tends to fray, use fray check or white glue on the edges. Glue the wings together in pairs. Fold and glue the lower edges under, reversing one wing. Glue one wing to the front of the angel and the other to the back as shown.

7. Hair: Wind 3 yards of yarn evenly along a pencil. Hand-sew the strands together on one side to form a row of loops. Slip the loops off the pencil. Pin one end to the center back and spiral the hair to cover the back, top and sides of the head. Sew or glue the hair in place. Wrap a band of gold ribbon around the hair; sew the ends together at the back of the head.

8. Face: Using 2 strands of thread, with small straight stitches, sew black eyes and a red V-shaped mouth. Brush blush on the cheeks.

Fabric painting is fun, but you should practice making smooth lines and clean dots, for best results. Always start the paint flow from the squeeze bottle on scrap paper, to prevent spritzing the fabric. Angle the nozzle on the fabric and move from left to right to make the line, squeezing the bottle evenly as you go. Don't push the tip back into the wet paint. To make a dot, squeeze a dot of paint onto the surface and lift the tip straight up. A peak will form, but it will eventually blend in.

Christmas Curtain

We supply simple patterns for the appliqués on this curtain, but it could be an ideal place to show off children's designs. After it has been easily slipped off the tension rod for storage, you could replace it with a curtain appliquéd with springtime motifs or any local themes.

HOW TO MAKE IT

1. To make a curtain: Turn ½ inch to the back twice on the side edges of your curtain fabric and stitch. At the upper edge, turn under ½ inch, then 2¼ inches. Stitch across the fabric 1 inch and 2 inches from the top to make a 1-inch-wide rod pocket and ruffle (adjust the pocket width to fit your curtain rod, if necessary). At the lower edge, turn under ¼ inch, then 3 inches, and sew or machine-stitch a hem.

2. Trace appliqué patterns: Trace the snowman, tree, and hat, and star on page 13, or trace drawings done by family members. Draw stars freehand or trace one from page 178.

*T*urn bare windows into festive visions with a star-struck Christmas Curtain. It will look good all winter. And it goes up in a flash because the appliqués don't require a stitch—you just iron them in place.

3. Cut the appliqués from the fabric: Following the manufacturer's directions, iron fusible bonding web to the back of the appliqué fabrics, leaving the paper backing on the web. Trace the patterns facedown on the backing. Cut out the fabric shapes.

4. Fuse the cutouts to the curtain: Pin the cutouts in a random but balanced manner across the curtain. (Hold the curtain up or hang it to view the arrangement.) Then mark the positions lightly with pencil or chalk. Remove the designs. Peel off the backing and fuse the appliqués to the curtain, following the web manufacturer's directions for proper heat and timing. Cut ribbons or fabrics for scarves and fuse them to snowmen's necks.

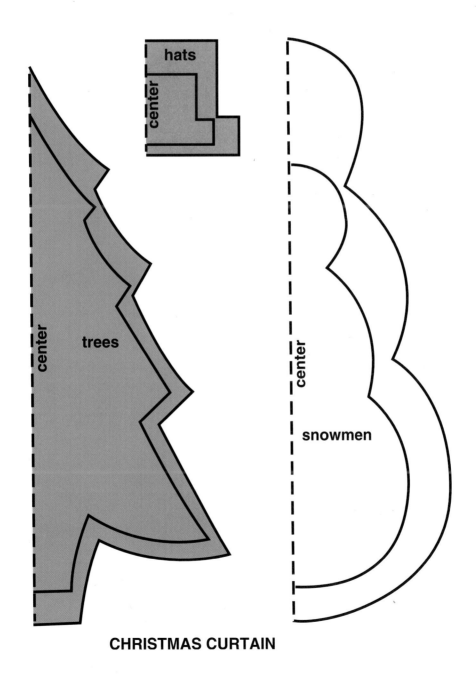

CHRISTMAS CURTAIN

These delightful Santas are designed to be cut in multiples from pieced strips of fabric. They make wonderful gifts, home decorations, or toys and could be best-sellers at a bazaar.

Santa Dolls

These dolls have wired arms and legs, so you can wrap them around banisters, let them tumble around on a tree, or have them hold hands to make a swag.

SIZE

14 inches tall

WHAT YOU'LL NEED (FOR 6)

- ◆ ¼ yard each of 2 different plaid fabrics and 1 yard of black 45-inch-wide cotton fabric for the bodies, arms, and legs
- ◆ ⅛ yard medium-weight muslin for the faces
- ◆ ⅛ yard white, low-pile fleece for the beards
- ◆ 24 wired 12-inch chenille stems to support the arms and legs
- ◆ six ¼-inch white pompoms, wooden beads, or flesh-color oven-hardening modeling clay for the noses
- ◆ 2 yards of ¼-inch-wide black satin ribbon for the belts
- ◆ gold metallic fabric paint (Folk Art Pure Gold) for the belt buckles
- ◆ black dimensional fabric paint for the eyes
- ◆ blush makeup
- ◆ fine paintbrush to paint the belt buckles
- ◆ polyester fiberfill stuffing
- ◆ white beans or Poly-Fil Poly-Pellets for weight
- ◆ low-temperature glue gun or fabric glue
- ◆ tracing paper
- ◆ masking tape

HOW TO MAKE THEM

Stitching note: To sew the seams, pin the fabric pieces with the right sides together. To stitch, guide the fabric edge carefully along the ¼-inch guideline on your machine (or mark a line on the machine with tape).

1. Preparation: Pre-wash the muslin and iron it while damp. Trace the beard pattern, page 16.

2. Assemble the fabric strips: Cut a 3¾-inch-wide strip across the full width of each of the two plaid fabrics. Cut a 2¼-inch-wide strip across the full width of the muslin. With the right sides together, pin the long edges of the muslin between the plaids and stitch together. Press the seams open.

3. Cut the bodies: Trace the triangular half pattern, page 16, to make a whole triangle. Alternating hats (pointed ends) and bodies (triangle bases), follow the Cutting Diagram, page 16, to trace and cut 12 triangles from the pieced strip.

4. Cut the arms: From each plaid, cut twelve 1½ x 5¼-inch strips lengthwise (parallel to the fabric selvage) to have 24 strips.

5. Cut the legs: Cut a 3-inch-wide strip across the full width of the black fabric for the boots. Cut the strip in half to have two 22½-inch strips. Stitch a black strip to the lower edge of each of the remaining pieces of plaid fabric. Trim the sides even. Press the seams open. Trim the plaid fabric to 4½ inches above the black fabric. Then cut twelve 1½-inch-wide strips lengthwise (parallel to the sides) from each panel to have 24 strips.

6. Assemble the arms and legs: Matching the color of the plaids, pin the arms and legs together, right sides together in pairs. Round off one end of the arms for the hands and the black end of the legs for the boots. Stitch the sides and bottoms, leaving the straight ends open. Turn the pieces right side out; press. **Insert the wired stems:** Fold each of the 24 chenille stems in half and twist the halves together. Trim 12 of the twisted pieces to measure a half inch shorter than the arms. The other 12 stems will be used for the legs. Wrap tape over the cut ends of all the chenille stems and insert the appropriate stems, folded ends first, into the arms and the legs. Stitch the tops closed, ⅛ inch from the raw edges.

7. Assemble the bodies: With the raw edges matching, pin an arm to each side on the front of one body piece of the same plaid, below the head. Fold the arms over the body. Place a matching plaid back, wrong side out, on top. Leaving 3 inches open at the center bottom, stitch the back to the front. Clip the seam allowance at the corners; turn the body right side out. Stuff the Santa, inserting beans or pellets in the lower 2 inches. Fold the raw edges of the opening inside. Centering the legs ¼ inch apart, insert ¼ inch of their tops into the opening. Sew the opening closed. Bend 1 inch forward for feet.

8. Faces: Cut the beards and the mustaches from fleece. Placing glue on the back of the fleece, glue the pieces to the faces. Paint black dots for eyes (practice making dots with the tip of the dimensional-paint squeeze-bottle first). Let the paint dry. Apply blush to the cheeks. **Noses:** Make small clay noses or sew on a bead or dye white pom-poms to flesh color in strong tea. Hot-glue the noses to the faces.

9. Belts: Cut six 10-inch lengths of black ribbon. With the fine brush and gold paint, outline a gold square in the center of each ribbon for the buckle. Let the paint dry. With a dot of glue, attach the buckle 1 inch above the lower front seam of the Santa's body. When the glue is dry, overlap and glue the ends of the belt to the back.

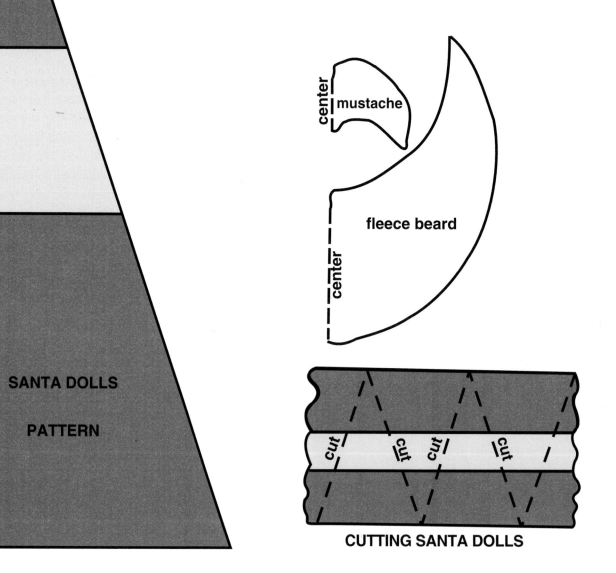

SANTA DOLLS

PATTERN

center

center | mustache

center

fleece beard

cut cut cut cut

CUTTING SANTA DOLLS

Jeweled, Painted, and Gilded Christmas Balls

Collect jewels and other shiny materials at crafts stores and flea markets. Make the ornaments at a crafts party or in a crafts class. They're easy to do, and working with others will spark the imagination.

BEFORE YOU BEGIN

Set up a place to hang the balls to let the paint or glue dry. You can prop them in paper cups or hang them from a tension curtain rod. Paint only half the ball at a time, if necessary. Hold balls at the bottom and make sure the caps are on tight before you hang them.

Ball with a Button

WHAT YOU'LL NEED

- glass Christmas balls
- gold glitter craft paints, both brush-on and dimensional writers
- faux jewels
- a large jeweled button or an acrylic jewel and mount (jewel enhancer)
- 24-inch-wire-edge ribbon
- paintbrushes
- tie wire
- gem adhesive or a low-temperature glue gun
- scissors to cut off button shanks
- ornament hooks
- pencil or felt-tip marker

I't's so easy to decorate Christmas balls like these, once you get going it's hard to stop. Gather materials and make them with friends.

HOW TO MAKE THEM

1. **Paint:** Paint a Christmas ball with two coats of gold paint, letting each coat dry.
2. **Glue on the button:** Cut the shank off a large decorative button. Or glue a jewel to a mount. Glue the button or mounted jewel to one side of the ball.

3. Paint dots: Practice making dots with the dimensional paint writers on scrap paper. With a pencil or fabric marker, make a row of eight evenly spaced dots around the button. Mark a second row outside, spacing dots between those on the first row. Paint the dots. Let the paint dry.

4. Make a bow: Fold ribbon to form a large loop and cross the ends at the back to extend from each side. Tie wire tightly around the center. Glue the bow in front of the hanger on the ball.

Bead-Wrapped Ball

- 2½-inch-diameter green Christmas ball
- acrylic, flat-backed jewels: twenty-five 7-mm amethyst smooth round jewels (cabochons) and twenty 7-mm pointed ovals (navettes)
- ½ yard string of 3-mm gold beads
- 24-inch or longer wide, glittery ribbon
- fine-tipped felt marker
- tie wire
- low-heat glue gun or gem adhesive

HOW TO MAKE IT

1. Draw lines on the ball: With the marker, draw eight evenly-spaced vertical lines on the ball.

2. Glue on the jewels: Following the photograph, glue stones to every other line, alternating cabochons and navettes. Glue the beads to the skipped lines. Add a cabochon at center bottom.

3. Make a bow: Fold the ribbon back and forth to form loops. Tie the center tightly with wire. Tie the wire ends to the hanging loop.

Ball with Gilded Lines

WHAT YOU'LL NEED

- ◆ a clear glass Christmas ball
- ◆ gold Press & Peel Foil and Foil Bond (from Royal Coat Decoupage Foil Kit by Plaid Enterprises)
- ◆ paper clip
- ◆ small, soft paintbrush to whisk away foil
- ◆ scissors

Note: Instead of using the foil and foil bond, you can paint lines with dimensional craft or fabric paint.

HOW TO MAKE IT

1. Apply lines to the ball: Start the flow of the foil bond from the squeeze bottle on a piece of paper, then make a random, flowing line of the liquid on the ball. Prop the ball to dry for twenty-four hours, or until the liquid cures clear, firm and sticky.

2. Gild the lines: Unroll some foil and cut a 1 x 2-inch strip. Lay the strip shiny-side-up over the ball. Press the foil onto the lines with your fingers and use the round end of the paper clip to press the foil along the base of the lines. Peel off the backing. Whisk away stray flakes of foil with a small brush.

*M*aking this garland and the ornaments could keep your child or a whole classroom busy for hours.

Snowman Garland, Popcorn Rings, and Doily Disks

Collect any shiny or bright trinkets you can easily find to decorate the snowmen and doilies. Stickers, jewels, snaps, and paper clips are a few we didn't use, but you can.

Garland

WHAT YOU'LL NEED

- several yards of ½-inch-wide ribbon the length for garland, plus 16 inches for tying
- 4 x 12-inch sheet of white paper for a snowman to every 6 inches of ribbon length
- black and assorted colors of construction paper
- scraps of ribbon or cloth for scarves
- felt-tip markers
- colored ¼-to-½-inch pompoms
- tiny black pompoms for eyes (optional)
- twigs for arms
- sequins and buttons for decoration
- masking tape
- white glue or crafts glue stick
- tacky glue
- tracing paper
- stiff paper or cardboard for templates

HOW TO MAKE IT

1. Make the patterns: Let the children draw patterns, or trace the half pattern on page 22 as follows: Fold the tracing paper in half to fit the snowman. Placing the fold on the center line, trace the outline of the snowman with the pencil, omitting the hat and boots. Cut on the traced line through both layers, but don't cut through the fold. Open the pattern flat. Trace separate patterns for the hat, boots, and nose. Trace the patterns onto stiff paper or cardboard to make templates.

2. Cut the snowman: Fold white paper in half, large enough to fit the snowman with the fold at the top. Hold the template on the paper with the top of the head on the fold. Trace the edge of the snowman. Remove the template and cut out the shape through both layers, leaving the fold at the top of the snowman's head connected.

3. Decorate: Cut out **hats, noses,** and **boots** from various colored papers. Attach them to the snowmen with white glue or a glue stick and try to tilt the pieces slightly differently to give each snowman a unique personality. With tacky glue or the glue gun, attach **twig arms.** Glue on tiny pompom **eyes** or make dots for eyes with a marker. Draw a **mouth. Decorate** the front with pompoms, buttons, sequins, and markers. Glue on ribbon or fabric **scarves.**

4. Make the garland: Allowing 8 inches of ribbon at each end for tying and 3 inches between snowmen, "hang" the snowmen over the long ribbon and tape the ribbon inside. Glue the paper front and back together, if you like, with a dot of glue. Hang the garland on a tree, across a doorway, or in a window.

Popcorn Rings

WHAT YOU'LL NEED (FOR EACH)

- 14 inches of sturdy, flexible wire (20-gauge)
- popped popcorn
- 22-inch ribbon for bow
- pliers
- wire snips

HOW TO MAKE THEM

Bend the wire to form a circle, but do not close the ends. With the pliers, form a half-inch-long loop at one end. Insert the other end through popcorn, cov-

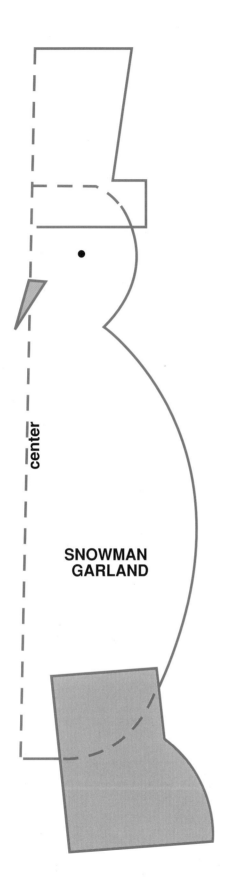

SNOWMAN GARLAND

center

ering all but the last inch. Interlock the wire ends. Tie ribbon in a bow over the joining.

Doily Disks

WHAT YOU'LL NEED

- 4-inch-diameter doilies or centers cut from larger doilies
- blue colored paper or assorted colors
- tacky glue
- buttons, star and snowflake sequins or other decorations, such as pompoms and stickers
- 12 inches of ⅜-inch-wide craft ribbon for each ornament
- drawing compass to make circles
- scissors

HOW TO MAKE THEM

1. **Cut paper circles:** With the compass draw 4-inch-diameter circles on the back of the colored papers. Cut out the circles with scissors.

2. **Add the doilies:** Glue a doily to the front of each circle with a dot or two of glue.

3. **Decorate the front:** Squeeze a little glue onto the back of a button or sequin and place it on the doily. The glue will seep through the openings and help to attach the doily to the paper as well. Glue on decorations at random or in the center of circles in the doily pattern.

4. **Make a hanging loop:** Cut a ½-inch-wide slit for the ribbon about ⅜ inch from the edge. Slip a 12-inch-long ribbon through the slit and tie or glue the ends together.

Angel Dolls

Instead of using velvet, you could dress these dolls in any leftover fabric you have. If you can't find small instruments they can hold, you can make some from cardboard or clay and paint them gold.

6 inches tall

- ¼ yard each of velvet, muslin and gold tissue lamé
- ¾ yard 20-inch-wide woven interfacing
- curly doll's hair (from a crafts store)
- scraps of Battenberg or other lace
- 48 inches of gold cord or pearls for head-bands
- six 12-inch wired chenille stems (pipe cleaners)
- ½ yard assorted narrow trims for neck and front, for each angel

*Y*ou could decorate a whole tree with these little angels, a garland as shown, or just prop one in the corner of a shelf to spread good will.

- miniature (2-inch) musical instrument for the angel to hold
- fine felt-tip permanent black marker
- blush makeup for cheeks
- polyester fiberfill stuffing
- fabric glue or low-temperature glue gun
- 8-squares-per-inch graph paper
- gold thread for embroidery (optional)
- thin, stiff wire for hanging

HOW TO MAKE THEM

Stitching note: Stitch seams with pieces placed right sides together using a ¼-inch seam allowance.

1. Patterns: Trace the half patterns for the head and body and the wing pattern. Draw a 1½ x 4-inch pattern for arms on the graph paper.

2. Cutting: For each angel, cut 2 heads from the muslin. Cut 2 bodies and 2 arms from velvet, with the smooth surface of the nap downward (see the tip on page 25). Cut 4 wings each, reversing 2, from lamé and interfacing. Baste the interfacing to the back of each wing piece.

3. Decoration: Embroider the front body piece with rows of machine or hand embroidery in gold thread, if you like. Glue or stitch a row of gold trim down the center front.

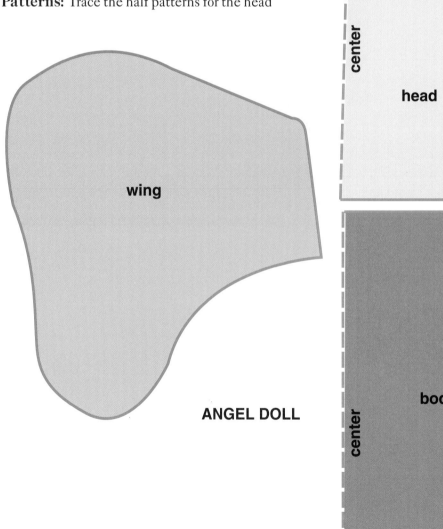

ANGEL DOLL

4. Arms: Fold each arm strip in half lengthwise with the right sides together. Stitch the long edge and one end closed. Turn the arm right side out. Cut a chenille stem the same length; bend back ⅜ inch at one end and insert this end first into the arm.

5. Head: Stitch a head to each body piece.

6. Assembly: With the right sides together, pin an arm to each side of the front ½ inch below the seam, with the raw edges matching. Stitch the back to the front, with the arms sandwiched between, leaving an opening at the bottom. Stuff. Sew the opening closed. Glue or sew trim over the neck seam.

7. Hair: Center a 10-inch-long bunch of hair over the head seam. Arrange, sew and trim the hair in a pretty style. Wrap and sew a headband of gold cord or beads around the forehead; lap and sew the ends at the back.

8. Wings: With the right sides together, stitch the wings together in pairs, leaving the straight ends open. Turn the wings right side out. Tuck in the ends. Lay out the wings with the center edges together. Cut lace slightly smaller than the front of each wing and apply the lace with dots of glue. Glue the wings to the angel's back.

9. Face: With the pen, draw dots for eyes and a curve for a mouth (make a pattern or pre-pencil this if you prefer). Brush blush on the cheeks.

10. Instruments: Bend the arms forward. Sew or hot-glue an instrument to the hands. Or cut two 1½-inch hearts from the lamé, stitch them together, stuff, and attach to the hands. Insert a wire or thread through the back of the angel to form a loop for hanging.

Tip: The direction of the velveteen nap (or pile) can make the color look different. To find the smoother nap of velveteen, brush the surface lightly each way with your hand. The smoother one will feel slicker. Be sure to lay out all pieces in the same direction when cutting.

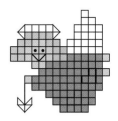

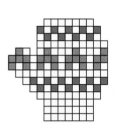

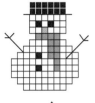
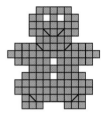

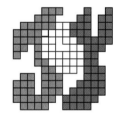

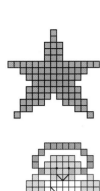
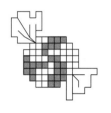

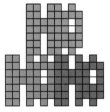

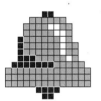

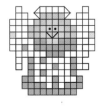

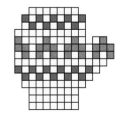

These little elves are working hard.
Christmas is on its way.
Please help them trim the tree
and soon....
it will be Christmas day!

1	2	3	4	5	6
7	8	9	10	11	12
13	14	15	16	17	18
19	20	21	22	23	24

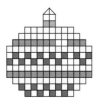
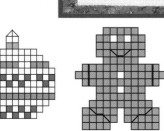
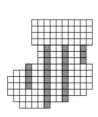

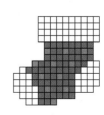

Cross-stitch Advent Calendar

Tired of making only cross-stitch samplers? Begin this project in late summer to have it ready by December. Children will love it, and it's sure to become an heirloom for future generations.

SIZE

11 x 18 inches

WHAT YOU'LL NEED

- white Aida cloth: 15 x 48-inch piece of 11 count for the background design and 10 x 14-inch piece of 14 count for the markers (amounts are exact; buy extra if preferred)
- red-print fabric: 12 x 19 inches to back the calendar and 11 x 19 inches for binding
- white-print fabric: 10 x 14 inches to back the markers

*S*tart with one of the cute little ornament markers in each numbered pocket. Then move them—one per day—onto the tree. It will be Christmas before you can say "jingle bells." Some cross-stitch and sewing experience is recommended.

- DMC 6-strand embroidery thread (2 skeins of green 230 and 1 of all others on the Color Key, page 28)
- tapestry needles sizes 20 and 22
- liquid needlework finisher or fabric glue and fabric stiffener
- Bond 527 Multi-Purpose Cement or tacky glue
- red Velcro Brand Hook and Loop Fastener, 12-inch strip or 24 Velcro Coins
- 12 x 19-inch piece of polyester batting
- red and white thread
- 13-inch dowel for hanging
- embroidery hoop

HOW TO MAKE IT

1. Cross-stitch background picture: Cut a 15 x 22-inch rectangle from one end of the 11-count Aida cloth. Following the design chart, page 28, hold the fabric lengthwise and mark the top corner of the dark red border 3 inches in from the top and sides of the fabric. Then follow the chart to embroider the design in cross-stitch, using 4 strands of floss in the larger needle and inserting fabric in the hoop. (Remove the hoop when not working.) Each square on the chart represents one square on the fabric. (For 2 colors in the same square on faces, adjust stitching accordingly, utilizing the center of the square to make half stitches to divide the colors.) **Note:** If you find the chart hard to read, you might want to enlarge it on a photocopier or use a magnifying glass.

Backstitch: When the cross-stitching is complete, with two strands of floss, backstitch black outlines and green lettering. Embroider the eyes with black French knots (see Common Embroidery Stitches, page 223).

2. Prepare the pockets: From 11-count fabric, cut three 7 x 15-inch and one 4½ x 15-inch strips. Baste a line along the lengthwise center of each strip to mark the top of the pockets. Then, starting 2½ inches from one end of the lower half, baste outlines for six consecutive pockets making each pocket 18 squares wide by 18 squares deep from the top line down. The side lines are shared.

DMC COLOR KEY

- background or white on markers
- black 310
- G - soft green 320
- med green 367
- lt green 702
- apple green 703
- bright red 666
- red 321
- X - dk red 304
- flesh 754
- pink 3716
- P - peach 353
- tan 436
- dk gold 783
- ▲ - brown 433
- gray 414
- burgundy 498
- green 701
- gold 725
- off-white 739
- orange 740
- lt gray 762
- lt yellow 3078
- ● - French knot, black
- O - Velcro dot
- — - backstitch, green 319 (lettering only)
- — - backstitch, black

These little elves are working hard.
Christmas is on its way.
Please help them trim the tree
and soon...
It will be Christmas day!

ADVENT CALENDAR

NUMERALS

Backstitch on markers:

striped stocking 701 (2 strands)
gingerbread man, white (2)
angels' hair 783
angels' heart 666
snowman 433
bows 666 + lazy daisy loops

3. Stitch the numerals: Following the numeral chart, page 28, with 4 strands of dark-red floss cross-stitch numbers 1 through 6, from left to right, centered in the boxes on one of the long pocket strips. Do not remove the basting. Cross-stitch 7 through 12 and 13 through 18 across the next two long strips. Stitch 19 through 24 across the short strip. Fold the strips in half lengthwise, right side out. Iron the embroidery facedown under a pressing cloth. Stitch the raw edges together on each strip.

4. Assemble the pockets: Center and pin the first pocket strip (1 to 6) across the embroidery, placing the fold ¼ inch below the script. With white thread, stitch along the basted bottom line of the pockets. Pin the folded edge of the next strip along the stitched line at the bottom of the previous strip, lining up the basted side lines of the pockets. Stitch across the bottom through all the thicknesses. Attach the remaining strips in the same way. Baste the ends of the strips in place.

5. Divide the pockets: Stitch through all the layers along the pocket sides. Remove the basting.

6. Add fasteners for the markers: Cut twenty-four ⅜-inch Velcro circles. Sew the hook halves to the embroidered tree, following the 24 circles on the design chart.

7. Backing: Starting 1 inch outside the top and sides of the design, trim the embroidered panel to about 11 x 18 inches. Lay out the back and embroidery right sides out with the batt between them. Baste the layers together, keeping the fabrics smooth. Trim the edges even.

8. Binding: From red print, cut two 2¼ x 19-inch strips for side bindings. Cut one 3 x 12-inch strip for the upper binding/casing and one 2¼ x 12 inches for the bottom. Press under ¼ inch on one long edge of each strip. With the right sides and raw edges together, pin the unpressed edges of the side bindings to the embroidered panel; stitch ½ inch away from the edge. Press the fabric away from the seam; fold and baste it to the back, covering the seam. Topstitch along the seam on the front through all layers. Trim the ends of the binding. Apply the bottom binding, tucking the ends in when you fold the binding back. Apply the top binding as for the bottom, but slip-stitch the folded edge of the excess to the back, leaving the sides open for the dowel.

9. Markers: Following the charts on page 26 and the Color Key on page 28, cross-stitch the 24 markers on 14-count Aida cloth with two strands of floss, leaving approximately 1 inch between designs. Use one strand for backstitch, French knot, and lazy-daisy stitches unless two are indicated in the Color Key. When all the stitching is complete, apply needlework finisher or fabric glue to the back of the design fabric and smooth on the white-print fabric. To stiffen the markers, apply finisher or stiffener over the backing and let it dry. Then coat the front of the embroidery (test on one piece first if using stiffener to make sure it dries clear). When the markers are dry, cut out each one close to its edge. Glue the loop half of a Velcro circle to the back of each marker. Place a marker in each pocket. Insert the dowel through the casing. Hang the calendar with the dowel resting on hooks or nails in the wall. Starting December 1, place one ornament a day on the tree.

Denim Angel

The pattern and materials for this ornament could be used as an appliqué on a T-shirt or a tree skirt. To do so, omit the cardboard and adhere the appliqués with an iron-on fusible web. Sew around the edges with matching thread.

WHAT YOU'LL NEED

◆ poster board or white cardboard; a 28 x 44-inch sheet cut in half lengthwise makes 12 ornaments

◆ ½ yard each pale-blue, lightweight denim for body and small-checked red gingham for wings (or sizes to fit separate pieces of poster board)

◆ scraps of calico

◆ 9 x 12-inch piece or scraps of white felt

◆ 2½ inches of flat gold cord for each halo

◆ 6 inches of ⅜-inch-wide red grosgrain ribbon for each hanging loop

◆ tracing paper

◆ clear spray adhesive

◆ white tacky glue

◆ black, fine felt-tipped marker

◆ sharp scissors

1. Make the patterns: Fold tracing paper in half. Placing the fold on the broken line, trace separate patterns for the angel's body, wings, face, and heart, below. Cut out the patterns through both layers, leaving the fold intact. Open the patterns flat.

2. Glue the fabrics to poster board: Trace the patterns onto poster board and cut patches of denim and gingham to fit. Following the manufacturer's directions, spray adhesive on the front of the boards and adhere the fabrics. Weight the pieces with books or magazines until the glue dries.

3. Cut the fabric shapes: Outline the patterns on the front of the glued fabrics and cut out the shapes with scissors or a crafts knife. Cut the face from felt and the heart from calico.

4. Assemble the ornament: Attach the wings to the back and the face to the front with tacky glue. When the glue has dried, make two black dots for the eyes. Wrap gold braid around the forehead and glue the ends of the back. Glue the ends of a 6-inch ribbon to the back of the head for the hanging loop.

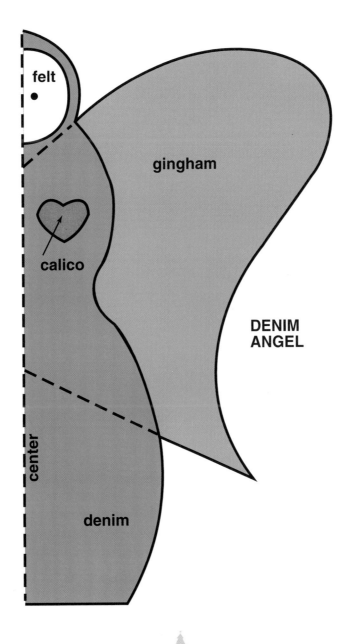

felt

gingham

calico

DENIM
ANGEL

center

denim

"Quilted" Christmas Ball

This is a good project to do at a crafts party or in a crafts group. Participants could each bring scrap fabrics, plastic foam balls, and a dinner knife. You provide the ribbons, pins, tea, and cookies.

WHAT YOU'LL NEED

- ◆ assorted fabric scraps
- ◆ plastic foam ball about 4 inches in diameter
- ◆ 24 inches of ⅜-inch-wide grosgrain ribbon
- ◆ dinner knife
- ◆ straight pins

HOW TO MAKE IT

1. Cover the ball with fabric: Cut a shape about 2½ x 3 inches from the fabric. Lay it on the ball and push the edges ¼ inch deep into the foam with the dinner knife. Cut a different shape to put next to it but with one similar edge. Start by pushing it into the shared groove on the edge of the first patch, then push the other edges into the ball. In the same way, attach patches of various colors and shapes until the ball is covered.

2. Add a ribbon hanger: Fold a 24-inch strip of ribbon in half. Using the two ends of the ribbon, tie a bow 4 inches from the fold, to form a bow with a hanging loop in the center. Attach the bow-knot to the top of the ball with two straight pins at angles.

You don't have to make a stitch to assemble this country-style ball. Just push bright fabric scraps into a plastic foam ball. It's fun to do and the results are truly eye-catching.

Lone-Star Ornament

You could use this ornament design as a quilt block, alternating star blocks with plain ones. Just make one layer, instead of two, and stitch the stars in place. Sew the blocks together and back the quilt with fabric.

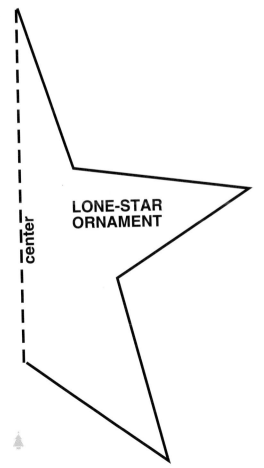

center

LONE-STAR ORNAMENT

HOW TO MAKE IT

1. Assemble the square: Place the felt squares back to back. Fold the ribbon in half and pin ¾ inch of it at the ends between the squares at the center of one side to make the hanging loop. Topstitch the squares together ¼ inch from the edges. Trim the edges ⅛ inch from the stitching.

2. Make the star pattern: Trace the half star, at left, on folded tracing paper, aligning the fold with the broken line. Cut through both layers, leaving the fold intact.

3. Cut two stars: Fuse web to the back of each calico fabric, leaving the paper backing on. Trace a star onto each backing. Cut out the stars. Peel off the backing.

4. Fuse the stars to the felt: Center and fuse a star to each side of the felt square, using a medium-hot iron or following the web manufacturer's directions.

Stars don't like to be all alone, so stitch up a bunch of these in bright felts and calicos to decorate a tree in a country theme.

*H*ere are some stand-up bears who'll add a whimsical touch to a mantel or table. Make them in small strips of three or four or in long, impressive rows.

Paper Teddy Bear Garland

This is another pattern with many potential uses. A single bear could be used as a fabric appliqué on a sweatshirt or a jumper front. Made a little larger, he could be simply cut from two pieces of tan fabric, sewn together, and stuffed.

WHAT YOU'LL NEED

- 18 x 24-inch sheet of tan construction paper
- 1 sheet each of red and blue rice paper (or other colored papers)
- ¼-inch blue dot stickers (or coding dots) for eyes
- white glue or glue stick
- fancy-edged paper scissors (optional)
- flat straightedge ruler
- crafts knife or sharp scissors
- tracing paper
- scrap of cardboard

HOW TO MAKE IT

1. Patterns: Trace and cut out the half-bear pattern, at right. Do not make a whole pattern.

2. Cut paper strips: With the ruler measure 6 inches down from the 18-inch edge of the paper in several places and make dots for a ruled line. Draw the line to connect the dots. Make sure the strip is the same width all the way across. Then cut the paper on the line. Use the strip as a pattern to cut other strips.

3. Fold the strips: Again measuring carefully, fold back a 2⅜-inch flap over the ruler at one end of the strip. Using the flap as a guide, fold the paper back and forth in accordion folds of the same width, making sure the edges are aligned before creasing each fold.

4. Cut the bears: Place the center line of the pattern on the fold of the first flap and trace the bear. The centers should be on an outer fold, the hands on an inner fold. With the paper folded on a firm cutting surface, cut through all the thicknesses along the outline with the crafts knife but don't cut through the folds. If you prefer to cut with scissors, or if you can't cut through all the layers at once with the knife, cut the strip into smaller pieces, allowing one fold for each bear.

5. Assemble the strips: Overlap and glue the bear's hands to join any short strips. Glue a small rectangle of paper to the back to reinforce the joining.

6. Finishing: For the scarf pattern, cut a paper strip to fit across the neck and another to fold for scarf ends. With fancy-edged scissors, cut the scarves from red paper for half the number of bears and blue for the others. Glue the scarves, folded as shown, to the front of the necks, alternating red and blue. Stick on the blue dots for eyes.

PAPER TEDDY BEAR GARLAND

Gingerbread-House Pillow

Do not be put off by the intricate pattern of the Victorian house. You can use the painting technique for any design. Make several pillows in related motifs to create a set.

SIZE

14 x 16 inches

WHAT YOU'LL NEED

◆ ½ yard brown linen fabric
◆ brown thread
◆ Shiny Fashion Fabric Paint (by Plaid) or another dimensional fabric paint in a nozzle-tipped squeeze bottle: 2 bottles of White and one each of Bright Red and Bright Green
◆ white transfer paper
◆ white tailor's pencil
◆ 25-inch square of smooth cardboard
◆ masking tape
◆ polyester fiberfill stuffing

HOW TO MAKE IT

1. Prepare the fabric: Prewash the linen, rinse it in cool water, and iron from the wrong side when damp-dry. Carefully measure, then cut two 18-inch squares from the fabric following the grain of the woven threads.

2. Make the pattern: Enlarge the pattern for the front, below (see How to Enlarge Patterns, page 220), or draw a similar design 14 x 16 inches.

Gingerbread-House Pillow   **Each square = 1"**

3. Transfer the pattern to the fabric: Place the fabric pillow front right side out on a firm, smooth surface. Center and tape the pattern on top, slipping in the white transfer paper facedown. Go over the pattern lines with a pencil or tracing wheel to transfer them to the fabric. Remove the papers. Strengthen the lines on the fabric with the white pencil if necessary.

4. Paint: To practice painting thick and thin lines, place the tip of the bottle at an angle on scrap fabric. Moving from left to right (from right to left for left-handers), squeeze the bottle gently and pull the tip along the pattern line. Never push the tip back through wet paint but start the paint flow on scrap paper to avoid spritzing the linen. When you're ready to paint the pillow, tape the pillow front to the cardboard. Start at the top and protect unworked areas with paper. Paint the white lines. Let them dry to the touch. (To speed the drying, hold a hair dryer on a gentle setting about 12 inches above the fabric.) Then paint the red and green lines and the green wreath.

5. Stitch: Trim the pillow back and front to 15 x 17 inches. With the right sides together, starting at the bottom, stitch the edges with a ½-inch seam allowance, leaving 6 inches open at the bottom. Clip the seam allowance across corners. Turn right side out. Stuff the pillow firmly. Turn in the raw edges and slip-stitch the opening closed.

Birch Snowman Family

The sawing is easy, and making the characters could be an evening's project for the whole family. Place the snowmen on batting (for snow) or among greens or potted plants.

WHAT YOU'LL NEED

- birch logs for bodies; ours are 3½, 3 and 2½ inches in diameter, but you can use any available sizes that will stand on their own
- twigs for arms
- dried currants for mouths
- raisins for eyes
- dried pineapple or papaya for noses
- acorns for buttons
- dried moss for hair
- materials for decoration, such as pinecones, artificial berries, a pomegranate, and dried orange slice
- strips of fabric for scarves
- glue gun or tacky glue
- drill
- handsaw or table saw for straight cuts
- pencil

OPTIONAL FOR A HAT BRIM

- scrap of ¼-inch-thick plywood, lauan wood, balsa wood, or cardboard
- coping saw, jigsaw, or scissors
- marking compass
- black paint
- paintbrush

HOW TO MAKE THEM

1. Cut the wood: Bodies: With the pencil, mark the log for the height of the body (ours are 9, 8 and 6 inches tall). With the saw, cut the logs straight across. Stand them up to test their stability and trim them if necessary. While you have the saw out, slice a 2-inch chunk off a thinner branch to decorate and use as a hat if you like. **Optional brim:** With the compass, draw a circle ½ inch larger than the log top on wood or cardboard. Cut out the circle. Paint the disk black.

2. Insert twig arms: Drill ¾-inch-deep holes for twigs about ½ inch above the midpoint on each side of the body. Dot glue on the ends of the twigs and insert them in the holes.

3. Faces: Tie the scarf around the body above the arms so you can estimate the space for the face. Mark positions for raisin eyes, a papaya or pineapple nose and a row of currants for the mouth. Remove the scarf. With a drop of glue on the back of each piece of dried fruit, attach the face. Let the glue dry.

4. Hats and hair: Glue the hat brim, if you've made one, to the top of the body. Glue (or nail) the wood chunk to the hat. Glue on moss hair. Glue pinecones, berries, leaves, and dried fruit on the top to make silly hats and hairdos.

5. Finishing: Tie the scarves around the necks.

With logs from the woods, a few dried fruits, and scraps of other materials, put together a perky family of tabletop snowmen to cheer you up all winter long.

Rickrack-and-Toys Wreath

If you don't have a lot of trinkets for the wreath, you'll find them in crafts and variety stores. Instead of using toys, you could trim the wreath with rickrack and lights. The rickrack will keep it bright when the lights are off.

WHAT YOU'LL NEED

- an 18-inch-diameter or smaller evergreen wreath
- 2½ yards each of red, green, and white jumbo (¾-inch-wide) rickrack
- assorted ornaments or small toys
- large pinecone (optional)
- a few yards of flexible wire or cord for hanging ornaments and securing ends
- wire snips or scissors
- wire for hanging loop

HOW TO MAKE IT

1. Make a wire hanging loop on the back of the wreath to establish the top.

2. Wind rickrack around the wreath: Starting at the back, wind white rickrack around the wreath in widely spaced wraps. Tie the ends together, or overlap and bind them together with wire. Repeat with each color, filling in the empty spaces.

3. Hang the ornaments: Hang toys or ornaments from the branches of the wreath with wire or cord. Wrap wire under the scales at the bottom of the pinecone to attach it.

Bright rickrack sewing trim adds lots of zip anywhere you place it. Tied around a wreath, it's a perfect accent for small toys or ornaments.

Natural Country Wreath

Cut as many pods, grasses, and berry branches as you can find in your area. Look for Indian corn and additional dried natural materials in crafts stores and garden centers. Arrange them on the wreath, striving for balance and contrast.

WHAT YOU'LL NEED

- an 18-inch-diameter vine wreath
- ¼ yard each red and blue calico fabrics
- 7 ears of Indian corn in assorted colors and sizes, including husks
- a large bunch of artificial red berries and leaves
- assorted dried natural materials
- long-leaf eucalyptus on twigs
- 5 miniature cowbells or large jingle bells
- a few strands of raffia
- florist's tie wire to make hanging loop and attached corn
- wired florist's picks
- pinking shears
- scissors

HOW TO MAKE IT

1. Make a wire hanging loop on the back of the wreath to establish the top.

2. Cut fabric strips: With pinking shears, cut 2 x 25-inch or longer strips of calico and tie them around the wreath, grouped on the right-hand side.

3. Corn: Tie wire or raffia around the corn above the ear and tie the ends securely to the wreath, placing ears as shown in the photograph. Make the husks part of the design.

4. Berries: Trim the stems of bunches of berries and leaves to lengths you can insert into the wreath. Insert a row of berries along the front and among the fabric strips.

5. Bells: Tie bells to the wreath with raffia or string.

6. Grasses: Fasten any fragile material to a wired pick and insert the pick in the wreath. Fill in the spaces with grasses, branches, and eucalyptus, inserting them so that the tips circle the wreath counterclockwise or in a harmonious pattern.

Make this charming country wreath when Indian corn is available in the fall. It will last through Christmas and beyond.

Mini Felt Snowmen

Make a lot of these and hang them on a tree as the main ornamental theme, or attach a few to the front of a wreath. Use them to decorate the top of packages or as table favors.

SIZE

5½ inches tall

WHAT YOU'LL NEED (FOR 5 SNOWMEN)

- 9 x 12-inch felt blocks: 2 white, 1 black and 1 orange, or equivalent scraps of felt
- two 16.4-yard skeins of green pearl cotton, size 3 (DMC color 909)
- embroidery or crewel needle-size 4
- ten 5-mm and fifteen 10-mm black pom-poms
- 2½ yards of ⅜-inch-wide red satin ribbon
- two 9 x 12-inch pieces of paper-backed fusible bonding web
- thin press cloth for fusing the web
- polyester fiberfill stuffing
- thin cardboard or stiff paper for templates
- tacky glue
- tracing paper
- sharp scissors
- pencil
- fine straight pins
- air-soluble fabric marker (optional)

HOW TO MAKE THEM

1. Make the patterns: Fold the tracing paper in half. With the fold on the broken line, trace the snowman pattern, below, on the solid outline. Cut on the outline through both layers, leaving the fold intact. Open the pattern flat. Trace and cut separate patterns for the hat and carrot. If you're going to make several snowmen, cut the patterns from cardboard or stiff paper to make templates.

2. Cut out the snowmen: With the fabric marker or pencil, trace five snowmen (including the

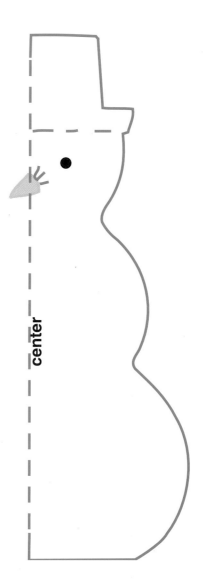

center

Make these felt snowmen by the bunch, put them in a basket, and let guests take one home after the party is over. Or make them to sell at holiday bazaars. Youngsters can practice their blanket-stitching on these.

hat shape) on the back (rougher side) of one piece of white felt. Pin another piece of white felt, wrong side out, to the front. Cut on the outlines through both layers. Turn the snowmen right side out in pairs and set them aside.

3. Cut the hats and carrots: Following the manufacturer's instructions, fuse web to the back of the black and orange felt, leaving the paper backing on. Trace five hats and five carrots onto the backing. Cut out the sides and top of the hats about $1/16$ inch larger than the pattern to overlap the edges of the white felt. Cut out the carrots.

4. Fuse the hats and carrots to the snowmen: Remove the paper backing and place a hat and a carrot on the front of a snowman. Cover the pieces with a pressing cloth and fuse them in place, following the web manufacturer's directions.

5. Embroider the carrot tops: Slip the labels off the pearl cotton, untwist the skein until it forms the basic ring and hang it somewhere so the thread doesn't tangle as you cut it. Thread an 18-inch length of the pearl cotton in the embroidery needle. Knot the end. Make 3 straight stitches above the top of each carrot for leaves. To fasten off, make two tiny backstitches (tacking stitches), one on top of the other, pass the thread under the stitches and clip the end.

6. Stitch the snowmen together: Thread the needle with a long strand of pearl cotton; knot the end. Working in blanket stitch (see Common Embroidery Stitches, page 223), start at the lower edge near the right-hand corner. Hide the knot between the layers and work the first stitch around the top layer only. Blanket-stitch evenly around the edge through all the layers, working 3 stitches from one hole to turn corners. Pause at the bottom to stuff the snowman, then finish stitching. To end neatly, pass the needle around the thread at the bottom of the first stitch and tack it on the back; bring it out between the layers and clip the end.

7. Finishing: Trim the backs of the pompoms so they lie flatter. Place a dot of glue on the felt in the eye position and press on the flat side of a small pompom. Glue on three of the larger pompoms for buttons. Tie an 18-inch length of ribbon around the neck. Trim the ribbon ends diagonally.

Tip: The blanket stitch is one youngsters can learn easily. These Santas, with their simple curves, are a good project for practice.

Trumpeting Angels

Brass sheeting for these angels is available in most hardware stores. If you can't find it, make the angels from cardboard and paint them gold.

SIZE

3¾ x 9 inches

WHAT YOU'LL NEED (FOR EACH ANGEL)

- 4½ x 10-inch .010-mm or .005-mm sheet brass or copper
- metal shears
- hammer, nail, and scrap of wood to punch holes

- ½ yard of ¼- or ⅜-inch-wide ribbon for hanging the angel
- thin cardboard or heavy paper to make a template
- crafts knife
- small, sharp scissors
- tracing paper
- light-bonding clear tape
- adhesive tape or tacks to hang from window

*T*hese angels are easy to cut from thin metal sheets and when hung cast an especially heavenly glow as they reflect lights on a tree or daylight through a window.

1. Make the pattern: Trace the pattern, at right, and cut it out with scissors. Tape the pattern to cardboard or stiff paper and trace around it. Remove the pattern. To cut, place it on wood or scrap cardboard and cut on the outlines with the craft knife. Cut the paper shape with the scissors. Poke a hole with the knife to start the cutout section between the arm and face and to indicate the position of the hole for the hanging loop.

2. Cut the angel from the metal: Trace the template onto the brass sheet with a pencil. Cut it out with metal shears. To cut the inner shape, punch a hole with hammer and nail to insert the shears. Punch a hole for ribbon at the black dot.

3. Insert ribbon for hanging: Tie the ends together at the desired length to hang the angels on a tree. Or hang them from the window, attaching the ribbon to the frame with masking tape.

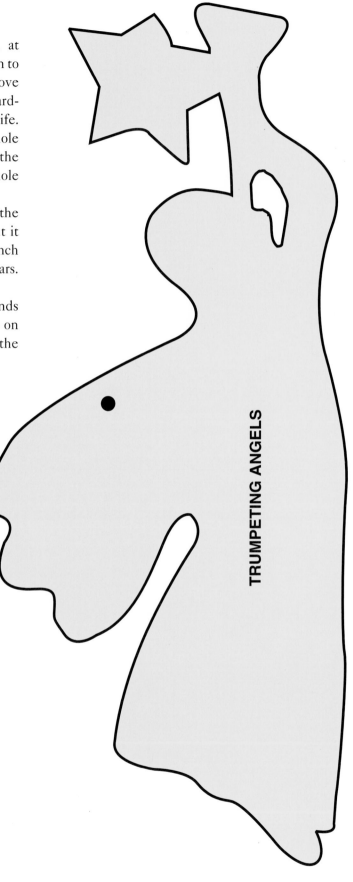

TRUMPETING ANGELS

Among all that glitters are handsome candlesticks made from balusters and metal leaf.

Gilded Candlesticks

Metal leaf is available in crafts stores and some art-supply stores. Less expensive and easier to work with than real gold leaf, it also can be used to brighten up boxes, flower pots, frames, trays, and whatever else you can think of.

WHAT YOU'LL NEED (FOR EACH ONE)

- a wooden baluster from a lumberyard
- white water-based primer
- FolkArt Barn-Red or similar red acrylic paint for the undercoat
- Dutch Metal gold leaf
- Mod Podge sealer/glue or white glue and a water-based clear finish
- saw
- drill with a Forstner bit to make a hole for the candle (or plan to attach candle to the top with glue or melted wax)
- flat paintbrush

HOW TO MAKE IT

1. **Cut the wood:** Cut the baluster to the desired height for the candlestick. You can trim the base shorter if you like, but make sure it's flat. Drill a ¾-inch-deep hole in the center top wide enough for a candle, if you like.
2. **Paint the undercoats:** Brush primer on the candlestick and let it dry. Then paint the candlestick with one or two coats of red paint. Let the paint dry thoroughly.
3. **Apply the gold leaf:** Little by little, apply a thin coat of Mod Podge or white glue. Lift up a piece of metal leaf gently with your fingers and pat it onto the surface. It may crack and break, but the cracks are part of the appealing look. Continue to add the leaf until the candlestick is covered. Let the glue dry. Rub the leaf with a soft brush to remove unattached flakes.
4. **Apply a finish:** Brush on a coat or two of Mod Podge or another clear finish, letting each coat dry.

All of these delightful stockings are made from the same stocking shape with colorful variations. Stitch them to give as gifts or to sell at a holiday bazaar.

Four Felt Stockings

The Dangling-Stars and Little-Trees stockings are easy to make. The Pine-Woods and Snowfall stockings require stitching around appliqués and are more challenging.

SIZE

14 inches long

WHAT YOU'LL NEED

◆ fabric marker or pencil
◆ tracing paper
◆ sharp scissors
◆ thread to match lining and fabrics
◆ see individual stockings for other materials

1. Make the patterns: Enlarge the outline of the Pine-Woods stocking pattern, page 51 (see How to Enlarge Patterns, page 220). Include the appliqué patterns if you're making the Pine-Woods Stocking or one tree for the Snowfall Stocking. Trace the tree, page 50, for the Little-Trees Stocking.

2. Cut and stitch the fabrics (for all except Pine-Woods Stocking): Cut the stocking shape from the pattern. Fold and pin the outer fabric in half with right sides together. Trace the stocking outline on one side. Cut the fabric on the outline, through both layers, to have the stocking back and front. Cut the muslin lining in the same way. **To stitch:** Pin the back to the front with the right sides together. Leaving the top open, stitch ¼ inch from the edges of the sides and bottom. Clip into the seam allowance on the curves. Turn the stocking right side out. Stitch the lining in the same way, but leave it wrong side out.

Dangling-Stars Stocking

WHAT YOU'LL NEED

- ½ yard of green pin-dot or print cotton or cotton-blend fabric for the outside
- ½ yard of lightweight muslin for the lining
- eleven 2-inch squares of assorted colors of felt for the stars
- eleven 8-inch lengths of assorted ribbons
- fabric glue

HOW TO MAKE IT

1. Cut the felt stars: Draw the patterns for the stars of different sizes to cut from the felt squares. Draw the stars freehand or trace one of the smaller star patterns from the Stars-and-Stripes Bowls, page 178. Outline 11 stars on the felt and cut them out.

2. Attach the stars to the ribbons: Sew or glue each star to the end of a strand of ribbon. Pin the ribbons to the top of the stocking front, trimming the ribbons to vary the lengths.

3. Assemble the stocking: Place the lining inside the stocking. Folding ¼ inch under on the raw edges at the top of each piece, pin, then slip-stitch, the top of the lining to the stocking.

4. Make the hanging loop: Cut a 2 x 7-inch fabric strip matching the stocking. Press ½ inch on the long edges to the wrong side. Press the strip in half lengthwise, right side out. Pin the long edges closed; stitch ⅛ inch from the folds. Sew the ends of the strip together inside the back seam of the stocking.

Little-Trees Stocking

WHAT YOU'LL NEED

- ½ yard of sturdy off-white cotton fabric for the outside
- ½ yard of lightweight muslin for the lining
- scraps of assorted green-print cotton fabrics for the trees
- 6-inch square or scraps of dark brown felt for the trunks
- ½ yard of red jumbo (¾-inch-wide) rickrack for trim
- ½-inch assorted color pompoms for decoration
- paper-backed fusible bonding web
- 3-inch square of cardboard or stiff paper for pompoms
- fabric glue

HOW TO MAKE IT

1. Make the tree pattern: Trace the triangle on page 50. Cut the shape from cardboard to use as a template.

2. Cut the trees from fabric: Following the web manufacturer's directions, iron the web onto the back of the various green fabrics. Trace the template onto the paper backing and cut 15 triangles from the green fabrics.

3. Fuse the trees to the stocking: Remove

the paper backing and pin or tape the trees, evenly spaced at random, to the stocking front. Fuse the trees in place under a pressing cloth, following the web manufacturer's directions and removing pins or tape before you iron.

4. Glue on the tree trunks: Cut ¼-inch-wide strips from the brown felt square. Cut the strips into fifteen ⅜-inch lengths for the trunks. Brush fabric glue onto the back of the trunks to attach one below each tree.

5. Finishing: Assemble the stocking, following directions for Step 3 of the Dangling-Stars Stocking. **Rickrack:** Pin rickrack along the top of the stocking. Removing pins as you go, apply very little glue to the back of the rickrack, so it doesn't smear the stocking as you smooth the rickrack in place. **Pompoms:** Trim the backs of the pompoms to flatten them slightly. Position pompoms evenly spaced between the trees and attach them with dots of glue. **Hanging loop:** Follow directions for the Dangling-Stars Stocking, Step 4, to make the loop.

LITTLE-TREES STOCKING

Pine-Woods Stocking

WHAT YOU'LL NEED

- ½ yard each of red felt for the back, white and dark blue felt for the appliquéd front
- 9 x 12-inch felt blocks: 1 each brown and light, medium, and dark green for the appliqués
- seven ⅝-inch and ten ½-inch star-shaped buttons for ornaments
- 3 each ½-inch, ⅝-inch, and ¾-inch flat red buttons for ornaments
- thread to match blue and green felt
- red 6-strand embroidery floss
- 16 x 22-inch piece of paper-backed fusible bonding web
- transfer paper in assorted colors

HOW TO MAKE IT

1. Cut the stocking and appliqués: Place transfer paper facedown on the front of the blue felt. Tape the stocking pattern on top. With a pencil or a tracing wheel, transfer the stocking and appliqué outlines. Remove the pattern. Trace the appliqué patterns onto the front of the felt in the colors shown. Trace the snow in one piece to go behind the trees. Add ¼ inch to underlying tree and trunk edges. Cut out the felt shapes.

2. Stitch the appliqués to the stocking: Starting with the snow, pin the appliqués to the stocking front. Slip scraps of web underneath the felt and press with a warm iron to hold the pieces in place. Zigzag-stitch over the edges with matching thread and medium-size stitches. Tug the back thread to pull the front thread to the back. Tie and clip the ends.

3. Sew on the buttons: With red floss, sew star-shaped buttons to the treetops. Decorate the trees with stars and round red buttons.

4. Assemble the stocking: Trace the stocking outline onto the back of the red felt. Adding ⅝ inch all around, cut out the felt. Pin the stocking front, face-up, centered within the outline. With matching colors, zigzag-stitch the front in place, leaving the top open. Cut points in the red felt with scissors. **To make the hanging loop:** Cut a ¾ x 6-inch strip of red felt. Pin the ends together inside the top back corner of the stocking. Sew the ends in place.

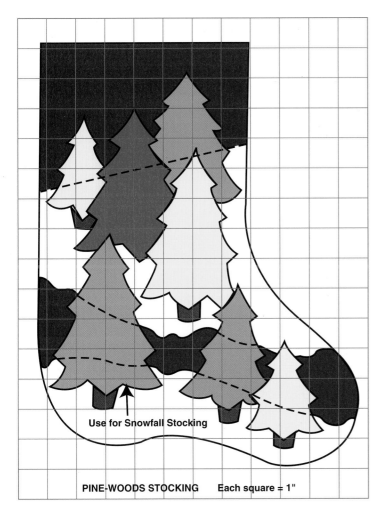

PINE-WOODS STOCKING   Each square = 1"

Snowfall Stocking

WHAT YOU'LL NEED

- ½ yard of red cotton or cotton-blend fabric for the outside
- ½ yard of lightweight muslin for the lining
- 5 x 8-inch piece of green-print fabric for the tree
- 2-inch square of brown fabric for the trunk
- 5 x 10-inch piece of paper-backed fusible bonding web
- Scribbles Snow Writer (by Duncan) or white dimensional fabric paint

HOW TO MAKE IT

1. **Appliqué the tree:** Following the manufacturer's directions, fuse the web to the back of the green and brown fabrics. Trace the patterns onto the paper backing. Cut out the shapes. Peel off the paper and pin the pieces to the center front of the stocking, lapping the tree over the trunk. Iron the pieces in place, following the web manufacturer's directions for timing and heat. Zigzag-stitch along the edges with matching thread.

2. **Assemble the stocking:** Follow the directions for the Dangling-Stars Stocking, Step 3.

3. **Add the snow:** Practice making small dots with the Snow Writer or fabric paint on scrap fabric. Dot snow evenly at random on the stocking front.

4. **Make the hanging loop:** Follow the directions for the Dangling-Stars Stocking, Step 4.

Sponge-Painted Country Stockings

If you're put off by the straight lines of geometric designs, try the overall star pattern on the red stocking at the right. Acrylic paint and textile medium are called for and easy to use, but you can use a flat fabric paint as well and omit the textile medium.

SIZE

13½ inches long

WHAT YOU'LL NEED

- ½ yard of Onsaburg or muslin fabric for each stocking
- 2-ounce bottle each of Christmas Red, Evergreen, and Thicket FolkArt Acrylic Colors
- FolkArt Textile Medium to thin the acrylic paint for use on fabric
- a natural sponge
- 1 yard of self-adhesive plastic shelving paper for the stencils
- red and green thread
- black medium-point felt-tip marker
- air-soluble fabric marker
- 1-inch-wide masking tape for stripes and taping fabric
- waxed paper
- coated paper plate or palette
- 3 small jars
- press cloth
- see-through ruler, rotary cutter, and mat (or straightedge and a crafts knife)
- scissors
- pinking shears

Cut stencils and sponge paint on muslin for stockings with a fresh country look. The technique is great for decorating place mats, curtains, or quilt blocks as well.

1. Prepare the fabric: Machine wash the fabric and press it dry while it's damp.

2. Make the patterns: Enlarge the stocking pattern, below (see How to Enlarge Patterns, page 220). Add a 1-inch seam allowance to the sides and bottom. Cut out the paper pattern. Darken the lines with the black marker. (To make the other stocking designs, trace the toe and heel or star of the design below and arrange them as you like or as in the photograph.)

3. Trace the patterns onto the fabric: Cut the fabric into two large pieces. Tape one piece face-up over the pattern and trace the lines with the fabric marker. Hold the fabric on a day-lit window pane and trace the stitching line on the back with a pencil. Turn the pattern over and trace the outline onto the other piece of fabric for the back. *Do not cut out the stockings before painting.*

4. Cut the stencils: Tape the edges of the pattern firmly over the front of the shelving paper. Mark the color of each section. **Red sections:** Working on a smooth hard surface and cutting through both layers, cut out the shapes to be painted red with the rotary cutter or crafts knife, leaving the 1-inch border intact. Place a ruler along straight lines when cutting. Cut out the stocking shape on the outer line. **Light green sections:** Remove the pattern carefully and place it on another piece of shelving plastic. Cut a

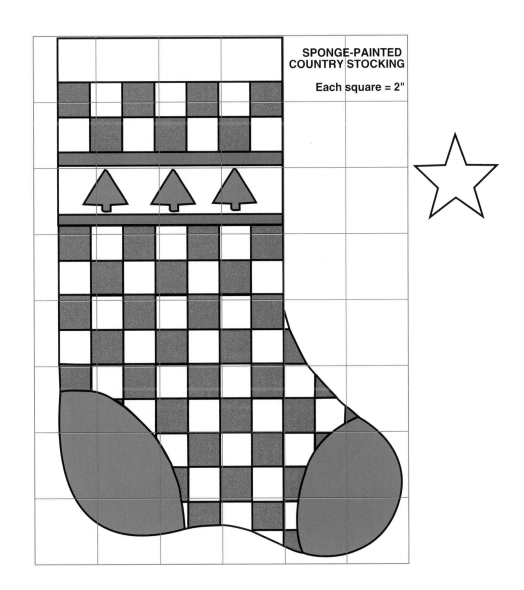

SPONGE-PAINTED COUNTRY STOCKING

Each square = 2"

stencil for light-green shapes. **Dark green stripes:** Cut a third stencil for the 1-inch-wide dark green stripes. **Stars:** Cut out stars to use as masks.

5. Prepare to stencil: Place the fabric stocking front right side out on waxed paper. Peel off the paper backing of the stencil for the red shapes. Carefully align the edges with the outline on the fabric and smooth the stencil onto the fabric. **Prepare the paint:** Mix the paint with the textile medium in jars, following directions for the textile medium.

6. Paint the stocking front: Red: Pour the red paint onto the plate or palette. Dampen the sponge and squeeze out excess water. Dip the sponge into the paint and blot it on a paper towel. Dab the paint lightly and evenly through the stencil onto the fabric to achieve a mottled texture. Apply paint more solidly around the edges to make the shapes clear. When the paint is partially dry, remove the stencil (you can speed up the drying process with a hair dryer set on a gentle speed). Meanwhile, wash the sponge. Let the paint dry completely. **Light green:** Position the stencil for the light green sections. Position the masks for the stars on the toes. Paint as before. **Dark green:** Using tape or your cut stencil between stripes, paint any dark-green areas.

7. Paint the stocking back: Cut a 3 x 7-inch strip of fabric for the hanging loop. Place the outlined stocking back and the loop piece on waxed paper. Sponge-paint the stocking back with the toe color and the loop with the uppermost front color.

8. Stitch the back to the front: Iron the fabrics under a pressing cloth, following the textile-medium directions. Cut out the stocking front and back on the outer line. Pin them with the right sides together and stitch on the seam line, leaving the top open. With pinking shears trim the seam allowance to ¼ inch. Pink the edge of the upper hem. Zigzag or serge over the pinked edges. Turn the stocking right side out. Fold and press the upper hem to the inside. **Hanging loop:** Fold the loop strip in half lengthwise, right sides together. Stitch the long edges closed with a ½-inch seam allowance. Trim the seam. Turn the strip right side out and press it. Pin the ends of the loop together inside the back upper corner of the front. With thread matching the color of the paint, topstitch around the stocking ½ inch below the upper edge, securing the loop in the stitching.

Patchwork Stocking

The patchwork design would adapt very well to pot holders, place mats, pillow covers, quilt blocks, and vests.

SIZE

15 inches long

WHAT YOU'LL NEED

- ¾ yard of red calico fabric for the stocking back, lining, and patchwork
- ¼ yard of green calico for patchwork
- matching thread
- paper for the pattern
- scissors
- fabric marker or pencil
- ruler

HOW TO MAKE IT

1. **Make the pattern:** Enlarge the stocking pattern, page 56 (see How to Enlarge Patterns, page 220). Add a ½-inch seam allowance all around the shape. To add the seam allowance, measure bit by bit and make a row of dots ½ inch from the outline. Connect the dots with a line. Cut out the pattern.

2. **Stitch the fabric strips:** Accurately cut or tear three 1½-inch-wide strips across the width of the red and green fabrics. With the right sides together, pin a red strip to a green strip on one long edge. Stitch the strips together accurately, ¼ inch from the edge, to make a strip 2½ inches wide. Press the seam allowances to one side.

3. **Cut the strips into squares:** Cut a strip into eighteen 2½-inch squares. Following the photograph for color arrangement, start at the top and lay the squares over the pattern, placing the seams alternately crosswise and upright to form the zigzag pattern shown. Once you understand the pattern, cut

*I*dentical two-color squares are cleverly turned one way and the other to form the zigzag design of the patchwork on this stocking.

enough squares to make the patchwork large enough for the stocking (it can be a rectangle).

4. **Assemble the patchwork:** With the right

sides together, stitch the squares together in horizontal strips with a ¼-inch seam allowance. Press the seam allowances to one side. Then stitch the strips together, matching seams, to make the patchwork. Press the seam allowances to one side.

5. Cut out the front: Pin the pattern to the front of the patchwork, aligning the top seamline with a horizontal seam on the patchwork. Cut out the front.

6. Cut the back and lining: With the right sides together, pin the patchwork stocking to the red calico fabric. Cut the back. Fold the rest of the red calico in half; pin the pattern to the front and cut around the edge through both layers to have two pieces for the lining.

7. Assemble the stocking: Pin the patchwork to the back with the right sides together. Stitch on the seamline, leaving the top open. Clip into the seam allowance. Turn the stocking right side out. Stitch the lining. Trim the seam allowance and insert the lining in the stocking. Turn under ½ inch on the raw edges at the top. Pin and slip-stitch the lining to the stocking. Make a loop from cord or fabric and sew the ends into the back corner as a hanger.

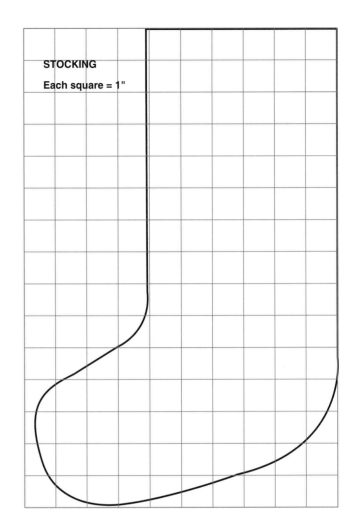

STOCKING
Each square = 1"

Tip: To make a fabric hanging loop, cut a 2-inch by 8-inch strip of scrap fabric. Press ¼ inch of each long edge to wrong side. Press strip in half lengthwise, right side out. Stitch edges closed.

Buttons-and-Bows Stocking

Dish towels are easy to use for this stocking, but any fabric you may have can be substituted. The buttons and bows are the main idea.

WHAT YOU'LL NEED

◆ 2 checkered or grid-patterned dish towels for the outside
◆ ½ yard of muslin for the lining
◆ 5-inch lengths of fabric and ribbons for the bows
◆ assorted, bright-colored flat buttons
◆ off-white thread
◆ scissors
◆ glue gun (optional)

HOW TO MAKE IT

1. **Make the pattern:** Follow the directions for the Patchwork Stocking, Step 1, on page 55.

2. **Cut the fabrics:** To cut the outer stocking, pin the dish towels together wrong side out. Pin the pattern on top. Cut around the edge of the pattern through both layers. Fold the lining fabric in half and cut out two stocking shapes in the same way.

3. **Stitch the stocking:** Pin the stocking front to the back with the right sides together. Stitch along the seamline, leaving the top open. Trim the seam allowance and clip into the curves. Turn the stocking right side out. Stitch and trim the lining, leave it wrong side out, and set it aside.

4. **Add buttons and bows:** Tie a knot in the center of each ribbon and trim the ends of the ribbon diagonally. Pin the ribbons and buttons to the stocking front, arranged evenly spaced at random. Sew them in place. Or, to glue them in place, place a sheet of paper inside the stocking. One by one, mark the

position with a pencil dot. Remove the button or bow, apply a dot of glue to its back, and replace it on the fabric.

5. **Finishing:** Insert the lining into the stocking. Turn the top edges under and slip-stitch the lining in place. Make a cord or fabric hanging loop and stitch it to the back upper corner.

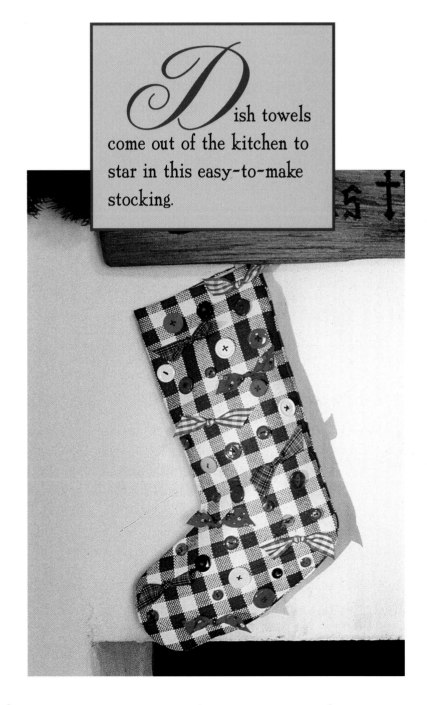

Dish towels come out of the kitchen to star in this easy-to-make stocking.

This amiable trio will spread good will wherever it stands among your Christmas decorations.

Pastel Cornhusk Angels

Look for dried cornhusks in crafts stores, garden centers, or Mexican food stores.

SIZE

About 7½ inches tall

WHAT YOU'LL NEED

- 9 or 10 dried cornhusks that are at least 4 x 7 inches in size for each angel
- dried corn silk for hair
- strong beige thread
- Rit Dye: pink, lavender, and green for the bodices and aprons and dark brown for dark skin
- white all-purpose crafts glue
- 6 inches of 20-gauge florist's wire for each angel
- wire snips
- spring-clip clothespins
- an acorn or 2 cotton balls to stuff each head
- paper towels
- glass bowls or plastic pails for the dye
- scissors
- ruler

1. Soak the cornhusks: Don't soak all the husks at once. Before you are ready to use dry husks, place them in a bowl of warm water for about three minutes or until they are flexible. Remove and stack them to use while they are still damp.

2. Cut and dye husks for the clothes and brown skin: Follow the manufacturer's directions and prepare hot dye baths. Lay the husks in the dye for several minutes until the color is slightly darker than you want it to be. Remove the husks and rinse off excess dye with cold water. **Clothes:** With scissors, cut two 2 x 6-inch strips of husk for each bodice and one 4 x 7-inch strip for each apron. Dye one set pink, another lavender and the third green. **Skin:** For each figure, cut one husk 2 x 7 inches for arms and two 3 x 6 inches for the head. Dye one set and some corn silk for brown skin and hair.

3. Make the angels: Use natural or brown husks for the bodies and heads. To fasten the husks in place, wrap them with thread two or three times, knot the ends together and trim.

Arms (one piece): Cut a 6-inch length of wire. Center the wire over one long edge of the arm husk. Fold the ends of the husk over the ends of the wire, then roll the husk tightly around the wire. Tie with thread ½ inch from each end.

Sleeves: Cut two 3 x 4-inch undyed husks for the sleeves. Lap a 3-inch side over one end of the arms, covering 1 inch. Gather and tie the husk around the arm about ½ inch from the end. Fold the husk back over the arm to reveal the hand. Tie the other end near the center of the arm to form a puffed sleeve. In the same way, make a sleeve at the other end of the arm.

Head: Cut two 3 x 6-inch husks. Tie them together at the center of the 6-inch length. Separate the husks at one end and fold them down in opposite directions to cover the tie. Stuff the head with the acorn or cotton balls. Tie again about 1 inch below the top.

Bodice: Insert the center of the arms between the husks below the head. Tie below the arms. Gather and wrap a colored bodice strip over each shoulder, crossing them at front and back. Tie around the waist.

Skirt: Cut five 6-inch-wide by 7-inch-long husks for the skirt. With the head and arms upside down, place a colored apron over the front covering the head, with its end 1½ inches below the waist. Add four or five natural husks around the body to form the skirt. Tie the husks slightly above the waist. Fold the skirt and apron down. Secure the overlapped skirt ends with clothespins to dry. When dry, trim the skirt even at the bottom. Trim the apron a little shorter.

Wings: Cut two 6-inch-long teardrop-shaped wings about 1½ inches wide at the widest end. Tie them together at their centers. Separate the wide ends for wings. Tie the wings around the waist, blending the narrow ends with the skirt.

Hair and halo: Let the angel dry. Remove the skirt clips. Glue corn silk hair to the head. Tightly twist a ¾ x 7-inch husk for the halo. Knot and trim the ends. Glue the halo to the head.

Finishing: Bend the arms forward. For one angel, roll and tie a narrow cone for a trumpet from a 3-inch-long husk. Fit the trumpet between her hands and glue the narrow end to her face.

Romantic Tabletop Tree

You will find dried roses in crafts stores, but they air dry easily as well. If you have a bouquet, it will dry in the vase if you let it. To maintain color, it's better to tie the stems together with a rubber band and hang the bouquet upside down in a dry, shady place until the blossoms are crisp.

WHAT YOU'LL NEED

- artificial tabletop tree
- terra-cotta flowerpot
- gold acrylic paint to paint the pot
- paintbrush
- chunks of plastic foam to fill the pot
- sheet moss
- dried roses on short stems
- a few rose leaves
- gold-edged ivory ribbon
- small, purchased foil-wrapped packages or a sheet of 1¼-inch-thick plastic foam, gold gift paper, and cord to make packages
- toothpicks to attach the packages
- tie wire
- serrated kitchen knife or a sharp knife to cut the plastic foam
- tacky glue or a low-temperature glue gun

HOW TO MAKE IT

1. Paint the flowerpot: With a damp sponge, wash the surface of the flowerpot and let it dry. Paint the outside of the pot gold. Let the paint dry.

2. Insert the artificial tree: With the knife, cut chunks of plastic foam to fill the pot securely. Wedge the foam into the pot. Push the tree trunk into the center of the foam. Remove the trunk, add some glue to the hole, and replace the trunk. Lightly glue moss over the top of the foam.

3. To make packages: If you don't have purchased packages, use a ruler and pencil to mark 1¼-inch squares on the top of the foam. Cut out the squares with a serrated knife to make cubes. Cut a 3 x 5½-inch strip of gold paper. Center a foam cube on the paper. Wrap the long sides of the paper around the cube. Overlap and tape or glue the edges. Fold the short sides in against the cube. Fold the top and bottom edges in diagonally to form points. Overlap the points against the side and glue or tape them in place. Tie the package with the cord.

4. Wind the ribbon around the tree. Start near the top and spiral the ribbon around the tree, bending it to flow gracefully.

5. Attach the packages to the tree: Insert a toothpick through one side of each package, near its base. Tie the toothpick to a branch on the tree with wire.

6. Attach the roses: Cut the stems 3 to 4 inches long. Bind them to the branches with wire. If you have a few rose leaves, wire them separately to the tree as well.

This dainty table tree with its tea-rose theme will be loved by grandmothers, mothers, and daughters alike. Make it from an artificial tree or adapt it to a natural tree.

Velvet-and-Gold Tree Ornaments

You'll find fabric, ribbons, and cord in large fabric and crafts stores. Be flexible. Work with the materials available. These are good projects to do with friends some afternoon.

WHAT YOU'LL NEED (FOR EACH ORNAMENT)

- a 3-inch or 4-inch plastic foam ball
- ¼ yard of velveteen or gold shiny fabric or another fabric to cover the ball
- scrap of muslin or tracing paper for the pattern
- ¾ yard each of jacquard, velvet, or gold ribbon up to 1 inch wide
- 3 yards of colored and/or gold cord, about ¼-inch thick, for the "cap"

- 1 yard of narrow gold braid and thin velvet ribbon (on uppermost ball) for trims (optional)
- ½ yard of ¼-to-½-inch-wide ribbon for the bow
- 8 inches of thin cord for a hanger
- a ⅜-inch gold bead
- straight pins
- Pritt Glue Stick
- low-temperature glue gun

*F*abric scraps and decorative trims can be combined for truly elegant ornaments. Make a bunch and add to your collection each year.

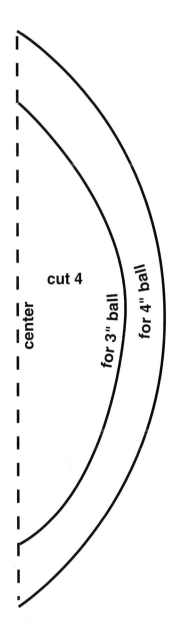

cut 4

center

for 3" ball

for 4" ball

1. Make the pattern: Trace the pattern for the quarter section to cover 4-inch or 3-inch balls, page 63, placing fold of tracing paper on center line. Test fit against the ball and adjust pattern size if necessary before cutting the fabric.

2. Cut the fabric: Pin the pattern to the fabric with the points placed along the bias. Cut four sections, marking the smoother direction of the velveteen nap on the back of each one (see the tip on page 25 to find the smooth nap).

3. Glue the fabric to the ball: Spread the glue stick on the back of one section of the fabric. With clean hands, so as not to get glue on the front of the fabric, smooth the velveteen (with nap downward) onto the ball, easing fullness to the edges. Place all the sections, butting the edges. Let the glue dry.

4. Add ribbon: Cut two lengths of decorative ribbon or trim to fit around the ball or slightly above where you want the cord cap to end. Use hot glue or tacky glue to attach them over the seams and crossed at the bottom as shown.

5. Make the cord cap: Poke a hole at the center top of the ornament. With hot glue or tacky glue, secure the end of the decorative cord in the hole. Little by little, apply hot glue to the ball and coil the cord tightly on the ball for the cap, ending above the middle of the ball. Poke a hole and glue the cord end into the ball.

6. Finishing: Glue the ends of an 8-inch thin cord into the hole at the top to form a loop for hanging. Tie a ribbon bow and glue it in front of the loop. Glue the bead to the bottom of the ball and secure it with a pin.

Tip: To find the bias (the true diagonal of the fabric grain), fold the top edge of a straight-cut piece down, even with one side edge. The diagonal fold formed shows the correct angle for placing pieces on the bias.

Hoop Lights

The wire rings for these ornaments can be found in large crafts stores or at a florist's supply store. All you have to do is push them together and wind the lights.

◆ 2 large metal rings the same size for each ornament (ours are 18, 24, and 36 inches in diameter)

◆ strings of outdoor lights (about twice the circumference) to cover each ring

◆ duct tape

◆ flexible wire for hanging

1. Connect the rings: Push one ring halfway through the other at right angles. Set them at any angle and secure them with tape at the intersections.

2. Wind the lights: Follow the directions for Outdoor Lighting, page 222, to wind the lights around the hoops. Hang the ornaments from the branches of trees or from hooks or nails on a porch.

These giant lighted hoops give a holiday look to elms, maples, and any other tall trees you have.

Daytime-Nighttime Bells and Balls

These oversize bells and balls are colorful porch ornaments by day. At night, strings of light give them extra pizzazz.

For real variety, let every member of the family paint one of these ornaments. Try hanging a few large jingle bells from the bell, to add sound to the lights and color.

WHAT YOU'LL NEED

- a 24-inch square of ¼-inch-thick smooth plywood for each ornament
- primer
- acrylic paints in assorted colors
- paintbrushes
- a string of 50 outdoor lights for each ornament
- duct tape
- sandpaper
- fish line or wire for hanging
- drill
- saber saw

1. Plan the placement: Decide how you want to hang and light the ornaments, referring to Outdoor Lighting, page 222. On ours, the light strings are connected along the garland, then to an outlet.

2. Cut the wood shapes: Enlarge the ball and bell patterns below (see How to Enlarge Patterns, page 220) or draw simple shapes to fit the plywood squares. After cutting, drill a hole for the fish line or wire. Sand the edges of the wood.

3. Paint with wood: Brush on primer and let it dry. Then pencil and paint simple designs on the ornaments.

4. Tape the lights to the back: Tape the lights to the back so they show around the edges. Hang the ornaments from nails, hooks, or porch brackets, as shown, with the fish line or wire.

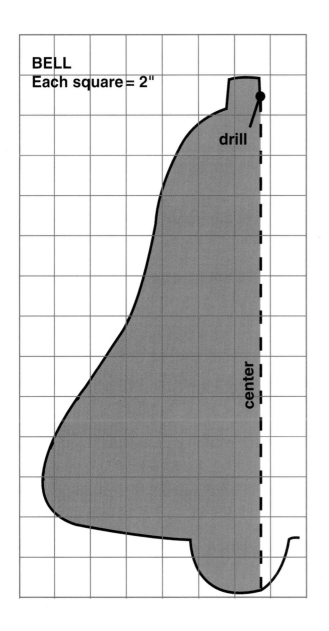

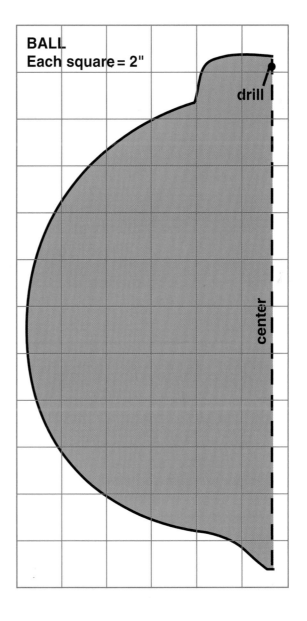

This familiar deer from the roadside signs looks terrific when lifesize in lights.

Deer in Lights

This dramatic yard ornament is one of our most popular. All you do is bend sturdy galvanized wire to the pattern shape, wind lights, and hang it up.

- 20 feet of galvanized 12-gauge wire (not electrical wire) for the frame
- 3 feet of 14-gauge galvanized wire for support
- additional wire for hanging
- strings of outdoor lights to obtain 200 bulbs
- duct tape or electrical tape
- plastic wrap
- pliers

- ◆ brown wrapping paper or newspapers taped together for making the pattern
- ◆ outdoor extension cord

HOW TO MAKE IT

1. Make the pattern: Enlarge the pattern, below, to scale on paper (see How to Enlarge Patterns, page 220).

2. Shape the outline: Lay the pattern on the floor or a large worktable. Starting at the rear foot, bend the wire back, with the pliers, to form a loop. Shape the deer, following the pattern outline. Grasp the wire with the pliers to bend it. To keep the wire from flopping about as you work, weight it with heavy objects or ask a helper to hold it down. Don't use separate strands of wire for the ear and the antlers; bend the wire back on itself to shape them.

3. Add supports: Hook the thinner wire across the shape on the dotted pattern lines to keep the deer from warping.

4. Apply the lights: Wind lights around the wire outline, following the directions for Outdoor Lighting, page 222.

5. Hang the deer out of doors: Attach wire for hanging to the top of the deer and wrap it around the branch of a tree. Extend additional wire from the tail and bottom of the deer as needed and attach them to other branches, or to the tree trunk, or to stakes in the ground.

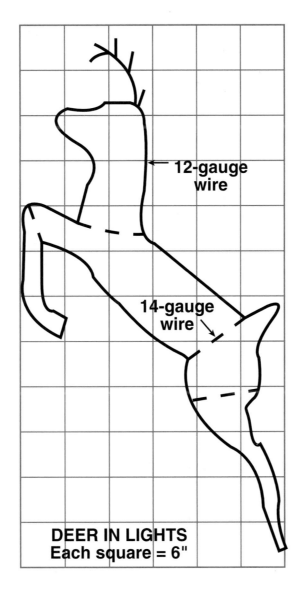

DEER IN LIGHTS
Each square = 6"

12-gauge wire

14-gauge wire

A flock of these red cardinals is spectacular on indoor or outdoor trees.

Cardinals on a Tree

Be sure to use exterior ribbon for garlands on outdoor trees. Wind it around the tree before arranging the birds. You could add little feeders made from scooped-out halves of oranges: just add a wire or raffia hanger and fill with birdseed. The rinds will dry on the tree.

WHAT YOU'LL NEED

- 4½ x 7½-inch piece of ¼-inch smooth plywood for each cardinal
- white primer
- red, yellow and black acrylic paints
- clear finish
- ½-inch flat paintbrush
- small round paintbrush
- medium sandpaper

- masking tape
- tracing paper
- transfer paper (optional)
- thin florist's wire for hanging
- drill
- saber saw with a narrow blade, or a coping saw

HOW TO MAKE THEM

1. Make the pattern: Trace the cardinal pattern below. Cut out the pattern and trace it onto the wood. You don't have to trace every cardinal separately; you can stack and tape rectangles of wood below the traced piece to cut several at once.

2. Cut the cardinals from the wood: Clamp the wood to your worktable and cut along the outline. Drill a hole for the hanging loop. Sand the edges of the cardinal.

3. Prime: Brush primer on the front and edges of the cut pieces. Let it dry. Prime the other side.

4. Paint: Transfer pattern lines for the wing and beak on each cardinal. Paint the front and edges red. When the paint is dry to the touch, paint the yellow beak. When the paint is thoroughly dry, paint the black eye and the wing line. Let the paint dry. Then paint the back in the same way.

5. Finishing: Rub the edges and surface with sandpaper to soften the color and create a folk-art look. Apply one or two coats of clear finish, following the manufacturer's instructions. Insert wire through the hole and form a loop for hanging.

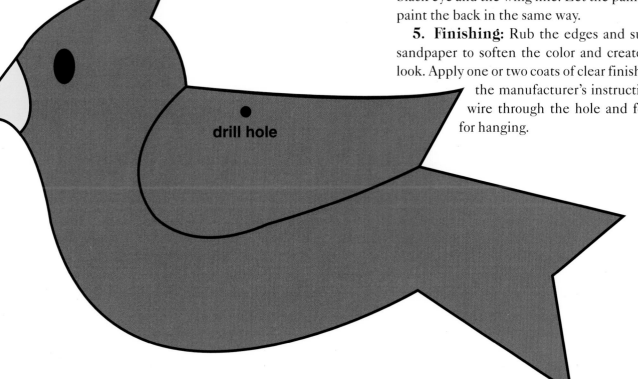

drill hole

Skating Santa

SIZE

About 53 inches tall

WHAT YOU'LL NEED

◆ a half sheet (48 x 48 inches) of ½-inch-thick
  exterior plywood, smooth on one side
◆ white primer

*This is an agile Santa. He can skate on either foot,
depending on where you attach the support.*

Plant Santa, a good
skate if ever there was one, on
a frozen pond; a snowy lawn is
just fine too.

- acrylic paints in red, light blue, dark blue, green, white, and black
- flat and round paintbrushes
- large sheets of brown paper or other papers taped together for the pattern
- masking tape
- hinge for the support stand
- saber saw
- clear water-resistant finish

1. Make the pattern: Enlarge the pattern to scale on paper (see How to Enlarge Patterns, page 220) and cut it out. Tape and trace it onto the plywood, turning it to fit on the half sheet.

2. Cut and paint the wood: Follow the directions for Making Wooden Cutouts, page 221, to make a support, cut the wood, prime and paint. After the flat paint is laid down, use mixtures of the same color with white to highlight shapes or with black to shade them as much or as little as you like.

3. Attach the support: Before you attach the support, notice that this Santa can skate on his front or back foot; choose one and attach the support accordingly.

4. Finishing: Apply clear finish to all surfaces, as directed by the manufacturer.

SKATING SANTA

Each square = 4"

Penguins on Parade

The fabulous penguins are easy to cut from plywood, and the painting is not detailed. They are a real eye-catcher, and you can easily have these little guys in your yard in time for the next snowfall.

SIZES

31 inches and 21 inches tall

WHAT YOU'LL NEED

- half sheet (4 x 4 feet) of ½-inch-thick exterior plywood, smooth on one side
- 8 feet of 1 x 2-inch wood for the stakes
- semigloss latex paints or acrylic paints in white, black, green, yellow, red, and blue
- 1-inch flat paintbrush
- size 8 or 10 round paintbrush for details
- wood putty
- putty knife
- sandpaper
- transfer paper
- 1-inch and 1¼-inch nails
- clear water-resistant finish
- saber saw or band saw
- drawing compass
- ruler
- pencil

HOW TO MAKE THEM

1. Make the patterns: Enlarge the pattern, at right, on a grid of 1-inch squares for the small penguins and on 1¼-inch squares for the large one (see How to Enlarge Patterns, page 220). Cut the patterns from paper and place them on the wood, leaving room for the pole, sign, and ball. Make paper patterns, or directly on the wood outline a 3 x 48-inch pole, a 7 x 10-inch rectangle for the sign, and a 7-inch-diameter circle (made using a compass) for the pole top. From the wood strip, cut three 20-inch-long stakes for the small penguins and a 30-inch stake for the large one. Cut a point at one end of each stake.

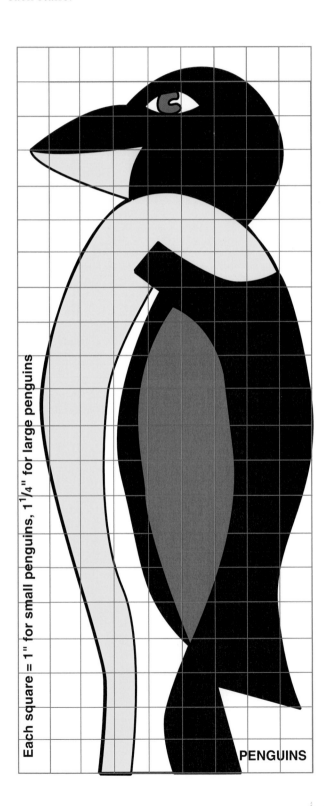

Each square = 1" for small penguins, 1¼" for large penguins

PENGUINS

Paint a family of South Pole penguins and send them north for the winter.

2. Cut the wood shapes: With the saw, cut the wood apart between the pieces, then cut each shape on its outline. Cut a point at the bottom of the pole and on one 10-inch edge of the sign. Fill the edges of the wood with putty if necessary. Let the putty dry and sand the edges smooth.

3. Paint a white base coat: Brush on two coats of white paint, including the edges but omitting the back, and let each coat dry. Using transfer paper under the pattern, trace the details onto the penguin fronts. Outline stripes on the pole with diagonal lines 1 inch apart. Outline "North Pole" on the front of the sign freehand in pencil.

4. Paint the colors: Paint the yellow and green sections of the penguins, including the plywood edges. When the paint is dry to the touch, paint the black sections. Paint the eye pupil and the ball on the pole blue. With red, paint stripes on the pole with the flat brush and letters on the sign with the round brush.

5. Nail the pieces together: Center a stake on the back of each penguin with its tip extending 6 inches below the bottom. Attach the stake with two or three nails through the back. Nail the circle and sign to the pole.

6. Apply finish: Apply two coats of clear finish as directed by the manufacturer.

Natural Stars and Heart

If straw is part of your life or environment, bring it out of the barn and into the light to make these handsome ornaments. For country folk only.

- precut plastic foam hearts and/or stars or a large sheet of 2-inch-thick plastic foam (from a crafts store)
- straw (from a garden center)
- a few yards each of raffia and ⅛-inch-wide red ribbon
- 1 or 2 wired florist's picks
- paper for pattern
- serrated bread knife or any long knife
- ruler
- felt-tip marker

1. Make a five-pointed star pattern: Trace the five heavy radius lines from the diagram, below. Extend each line to measure 7 inches and draw a 14-inch-wide star, following the broken lines from A to B, B to C, etc., and ending at F.

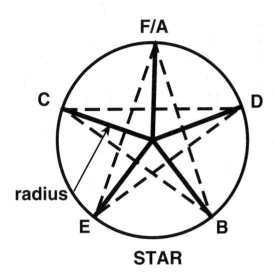

2. Make a heart pattern: Fold a large sheet of newspaper in half and draw the curve for a half heart 7½ inches wide by 16 inches long with its center on the fold. Cut out the pattern, through both layers. Open it flat to have a 15 x 16-inch heart.

3. Cut the heart and star from the foam: Trace the patterns onto the plastic foam with the marker and cut them out with the knife.

4. Cover the shapes with straw: Place the plastic foam shape over several long strands of raffia. Spread crisscrossed layers of straw on the front and sides of the foam until it is well covered. Let the ends of some straw extend beyond the tips of the star. Tie the straw in place by wrapping the shape every which way with the raffia. Wind and tie ribbon around the shapes at random.

5. To hang: Form a wire loop on a florist's pick and insert the pick downward firmly into the back of the foam.

*S*tars and hearts made of straw are perfect on a country-style porch.

*P*lain and classic, this rustic star will look good anytime of the year on an indoor wall, a porch, or even a fence.

Twig Star

The star is cut after you nail the twigs to plywood and paint them. The technique could be used for other simple shapes, such as bells, birds, or snowmen. We like the look. Go for it.

WHAT YOU'LL NEED

- 24-inch square of ¼-inch or ½-inch-thick plywood
- about thirty-three 24-inch x ¾-inch-diameter straight birch or other branches
- 1¼-inch nails or brads
- wood glue
- white acrylic paint
- paintbrush
- tracing paper
- saber saw
- sawtooth hanger or screw eyes and wire for hanging

HOW TO MAKE IT

1. Cover the plywood with branches: Saw or nip any side twigs off the branches. Glue and nail the branches side by side to the plywood, inserting nails from the back or front as needed. Pre-drill holes in the branches, if necessary, to prevent them from splitting. Let the glue dry.

2. Paint the branches: Brush a coat of water-thinned paint on the branches for a whitewashed look. Let the paint dry.

3. Make the star pattern: Trace the 5 heavy radius lines from the star diagram, page 76. Extending the lines to measure 12 inches, draw a star, following the lines in order from A to B, B to C, etc.

4. Cut the star from wood: Cut out the star with the saw. Hang it with sawtooth hangers or screw eyes and wire.

Lattice Trees and Deer Yard Ornaments

These trellises are worth the effort to make; you will have year-round decorations to define small spaces, back up gardens, or serve as focal points in a field. The lattice panels can be obtained in lumberyards.

Lattice Trees

Simple trees and deer cut from lattice panels make elegant outdoor trellises to decorate with vines or lights.

1. Cut the wood: Mark the tree shape on the lattice panel, following the diagram below, or make it any size you like. Cut out the shape. Cut lattice strips to edge the back and front, mitering the corners at the top point. Cut the lower edge of the trunk with points you can stick into the ground.

2. Frame the edges: Glue the border strips over the edges of the tree front and back and nail each end to hold them in place. Then nail them over each end of the lattice.

3. Paint: Thin the paint with 2 parts water to make a stain. (Test on scrap wood and adjust the por portions if necessary.) Apply the stain to both sides of the wood. When the paint is dry, apply the finish, following the manufacturer's directions.

4. Install the trees in the ground: Push the stakes at the bottom into the ground. Push separate stakes into the ground as needed and tie the ornament with wire to the stakes for support. Weave vines through the lattice at random. Wire pinecones and berries to the vines.

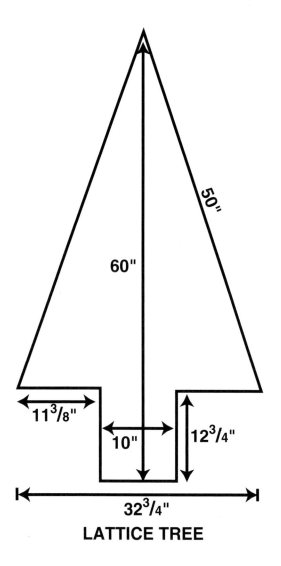

LATTICE TREE

Lattice Deer

SIZE

32 x 48 inches

WHAT YOU'LL NEED

- 4-foot x 4-foot x ¼-inch-thick (or thicker) lattice panel with ¾-inch spaces or lattice with wider spaces reinforced with extra lattice strips. Note: The lattice grid must be small enough to define the deer shape. We used lattice with 2¾-inch spaces and glued and stapled 1½-inch-wide lattice strips in the spaces before cutting.
- 17 x 17-inch scrap of lattice panel with 2¾-inch grid (or 60 x 1½ x ¼-inch lattice strips) to make the antlers
- white and brown acrylic paint
- paintbrushes
- clear exterior finish
- vines, pinecones, and berries or outdoor lights for decorating
- large sheets of paper for pattern
- yardstick

- wood glue
- ⅝-inch brads
- staple gun and staples for wood
- stakes
- strong flexible coated wire

HOW TO MAKE THEM

1. Cut the wood: Reinforce the panel with wood strips as described in the materials list, if necessary. Enlarge the pattern, below, on paper (see How to Enlarge Patterns, page 220). Transfer the pattern to the lattice panel and cut out the deer. Cut antlers from the lattice scraps or build them from extra strips of wood. Glue and nail the antlers to the back of the head. Cut four 6-inch stakes with points at one end and nail them with points downward to the bottom of each leg.

2. Paint: Brush white paint lightly on the deer's belly, tail, antlers and the back of the hind legs. Paint the brown eye. When the paint is dry, apply the finish, following the manufacturer's instructions.

3. Install the deer in the ground: See Lattice Trees, Step 4, page 80, for installation. Tie greenery to the neck and add branches, vines, and berries as you like.

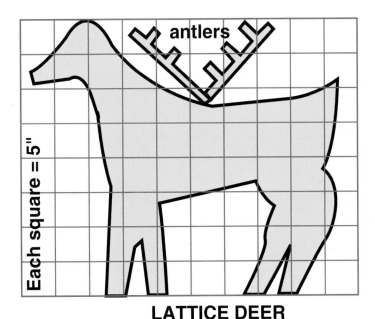

LATTICE DEER

Pine-Tree Doormat

This is a fun way to personalize a doormat. Simply outline the shapes with masking tape and paint with household sponges.

- bristle (coir) semi-circular or rectangular doormat
- blue-green, green, and yellow-green acrylic paints
- graph paper for patterns
- household sponge
- masking tape
- foil pans or coated paper plates for paint

HOW TO MAKE IT

1. Make the tree patterns: Outline triangles on the mat with masking tape (ours are 8 x 11 inches and 5 x 6½ inches), allowing at least 4 inches below them for the trunks and white border. An easy way to make a pattern is to cut a rectangle of paper the desired height and width of the triangle. Fold the paper in half lengthwise and cut from the lower outer corner to the top of the fold. Open the paper flat.

2. Paint the trees: From a slightly damp sponge cut 1½-inch squares for painting. Save one for white paint. Pour paint into the pans and with a sponge, paint each tree a different shade of green. Paint a 1½-inch yellow-green square centered about ½ inch below each tree for the trunks.

3. Paint the border: With the clean sponge, print white squares about 1½ inches apart along the mat edge. Let the paint dry.

This decorated mat is easy to make and well worth the effort. Paint it for the holidays and enjoy it for years after.

A set of jingle bells on the front door will sound as festive as they look.

Birch-Log Doorbells

This cheerful door ornament can be made just as successfully with any local wood or a painted dowel. The main thing is to let it jingle.

WHAT YOU'LL NEED

- 13-inch-long thin birch log
- six 2-inch and two 1-inch jingle bells
- 3 yards of ⅞-inch-wide red grosgrain ribbon
- artificial or natural berries
- 2 pinecones
- staple gun or nails
- drill
- glue gun

HOW TO MAKE IT

Note: Slice the back of the log flat if necessary.

1. Drill holes for ribbon handle: Mark a straight line across the log to define the top. Make a dot on the line 1 inch from each end of the log. At each dot drill a ⅜-inch-diameter hole diagonally outward to the center of the cut end of the log. **Note:** If using a dowel, don't drill holes. Plan to tie or staple the ribbon handle in place.

2. Thread the ribbon through the holes: Thread the ends of a 24-inch-long ribbon down through the holes and tie a small bell to each end of the ribbon. To thread the ribbon easily, wrap the tip with masking tape.

3. Add the dangling bells: Cut three 13-inch and three 15-inch lengths of ribbon. Tie a bell to one end of each strip. Nail or staple the free ends of the ribbon to the back of the log, alternating lengths.

4. Attach pinecones: Glue pinecones and berries to the top of the log.

VALENTINE'S DAY

Don't forget your friends

Make-a-Memory Pillow

♥

If you're not the lacy, romantic type, make the pillow with any kind of memorabilia—bits of old clothing, symbolic appliqués, jewelry—whatever.

SIZE

9-inch square

WHAT YOU'LL NEED

◆ two 10-inch squares of pink (or any color) cotton or other fabric for a 9 x 9-inch pillow

◆ a snapshot

◆ ½- or ¾-inch-wide flat lace to frame the snapshot

◆ lace trims, scraps, and/or doilies

◆ assorted memorabilia, such as charms, old buttons, earrings, pins, or a string of pearls or beads

◆ ½ yard of ⅜-inch-wide satin ribbon

◆ a few purchased ribbon roses

◆ thread to match fabric and laces

◆ polyester fiberfill stuffing

- fabric glue or a low-temperature glue gun
- 5 x 10-inch or larger paper for pattern

HOW TO MAKE IT

1. Cut the fabric: Draw a heart pattern following the diagram at right. Fold the fabric square in half, wrong side out. Place the broken line of the pattern on the fold and pin the pattern in place. Cut along the curved heart edge through both layers. Repeat with the other fabric square.

2. Attach the lace: Arrange the trims and doilies on the pillow-front heart. When you like the arrangement, pin the pieces in place. Trim the outer edges to match the heart. Then stitch, tack or glue the laces to the fabric only as much as needed to hold them in place.

3. Assemble the pillow: With the right sides together and ½-inch seam allowance, stitch the back to the front, leaving an opening at one side for inserting the stuffing. Clip slits into the seam allowance at the point and on the curves. Turn the heart right side out. Stuff it firmly with fiberfill. Turn in the raw edges and slip-stitch the opening closed.

4. "Frame" the snapshot: Place half the width of the lace trim along the edge of the photo front, folding the corners neatly and attaching only the corners and overlapped ends with a dot of glue. Let the glue dry. Fold the other half of the lace to the back and glue it in place as you did the front.

5. Add the memorabilia: Arrange, then glue or sew the snapshot, roses, buttons, trinkets, and string of beads to the front. Always use the glue sparingly. Fold three 6-inch-long ribbons in half. Tack the ends together with the loops slightly separated. Then tack the loops to the center top of the pillow at the back so they show in the front.

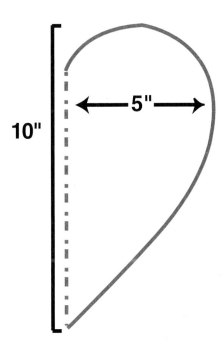

Dried-Flower Topiaries

♥

Make these potted beauties with your own dried flowers or others from crafts stores or garden centers. You could also use silk flowers. Just wedge florist's foam into pots, add dried moss, and insert the stems or glue the blossoms. Our designer filled the pots for the short topiaries with plaster of paris to give a nice weightiness, but you don't have to.

WHAT YOU'LL NEED

FOR THE TALL TOPIARIES:

- 4-inch-diameter terra-cotta flowerpot
- a bunch of long-stemmed dried flowers about 12 inches tall
- florist's foam

FOR THE SHORT TOPIARIES:

- 4- or 5-inch-diameter terra-cotta flowerpots
- about 20 medium-size dried rose blossoms or about 50 small flat dried flowers
- plaster of paris from a crafts or art-supply store (optional) or florist's foam

FOR ALL THE TOPIARIES:

- a small amount of dried sheet moss
- 1 yard of 1½-inch-wide wire-edge ribbon
- low-temperature glue gun

HOW TO MAKE THEM

Tall topiary: Cut and wedge florist's foam into the flowerpot, so that foam fills the pot to ¼-inch below the rim. Tie the flower stems together with ribbon as shown in the photograph. Trim the stem ends even. Insert the stems about 2 inches into the center of the foam. Glue on enough moss to cover the top of the foam.

Short topiary, using roses: To use plaster of paris, cover the hole at the bottom of the flowerpot with cardboard or paper. Then mix plaster of paris as directed and fill the pot to ¼ inch below the rim. Let the plaster dry. **To use florist's foam,** fill the pot with foam, to ¼ inch from the top.

Glue on enough moss to cover the top of the plaster or foam. Starting at the center, glue the roses to the moss, placing a dot of glue on rose. Place ribbon around the pot rim and tie the ends in a bow.

Short topiary, using flat flowers: Fill the pot with plaster of paris as for the roses, or florist's foam mounded ¾ inch above the pot. Glue a 1-inch-thick slice of florist's foam to the plaster. With a sharp or serrated knife, trim the edges of the foam to form a low dome shape on the top of the pot. Starting at the center, glue the flowers to the foam. Glue moss around the edge. Tie ribbon around the pot, twisting it at intervals, and tie the ends in a bow.

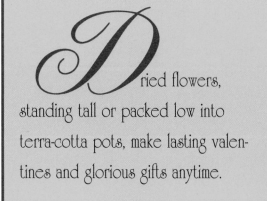

Dried flowers, standing tall or packed low into terra-cotta pots, make lasting valentines and glorious gifts anytime.

Love-Letter Desk

Decorate this lap desk for someone who prefers old-fashioned letter writing to E-mail. Stationery, pen, and correspondence can be kept together inside. It could be the place you designate to hold clippings, coupons, or crafts tools.

SIZE

10½ x 15 x 5½ inches

WHAT YOU'LL NEED

- 10½ x 15 x 5½-inch unpainted wooden lap desk (from a crafts store)
- white primer
- cream-color flat- or eggshell-finish latex paint
- dark green latex paint for the inside (optional)
- white and yellow acrylic paints
- floral pictures cut from gift wrap
- a small brass drawer pull (optional)
- ½-inch-wide drafting tape or painter's masking tape to mask the trellis lines

Treat a plain wooden lap desk from the crafts store to a diamond-bright painted trellis with decoupaged roses.

- Mod Podge matte sealer/glue
- clear satin water-based finish
- flat paintbrushes
- natural or torn household sponge
- fine sandpaper
- coated paper plate, palette, or paint pan
- a few sheets of paper

HOW TO MAKE IT

1. Paint the desk: Sand the desk lightly following the wood grain. Dust off the residue. Following the manufacturer's instructions for the primer and paint, brush primer on the desk inside and out, letting it dry with the lid open. Paint the outside with two coats of cream color, letting each coat dry thoroughly. Paint the inside cream or dark green.

2. Tape the trellis lines: Fold a square piece of paper in half diagonally to have a 45-degree angle as a guide for taping the grid lines as shown in the photograph. Starting at the upper left corner of the lid, align one edge of the angle with the top. Tape a line diagonally across the lid. Move 3½ inches to the right and tape a parallel line. Continue in this manner. (If your desk is a different size, measure to lay out an even grid.) Then start in the right corner and tape lines in the opposite direction to make the grid. Tape the short lower lines shown from the sides of the lid to complete the grid squares. From each end of the tapes, extend the grid lines straight back to the edge of the desk and down the front as shown.

3. Paint the diamonds: Following the photograph, tape paper over the trellis sections to be painted yellow while you paint the white sections. With a slightly damp sponge, dab white paint lightly and evenly on the uncovered sections of the trellis. When the paint is dry, remove the paper masks from the yellow sections. Then cover the white sections with paper, and sponge the uncovered sections with yellow paint. Remove the tape slowly. Retouch the paint with a small brush if necessary.

4. Glue on the flowers: Arrange the cut-paper flowers on the lid. Where you want flowers to appear to be behind the trellis, cut the edges straight along the trellis lines. Mark the positions lightly with pencil, remove the cutouts one by one and glue them in place with Mod Podge sealer/glue. Brush Mod Podge over the cutouts as well. Let the glue dry.

5. Finishing: Brush two coats of clear finish over the painted and decoupaged surfaces, again propping up the lid and letting each coat dry. Insert the drawer pull at the center front, if desired.

Tip: To apply paper cutouts, brush glue on bare backs. Hold them by the edge when placing them so you don't remove any glue and smooth them in place, pressing out air bubbles. Wipe off excess glue with a slightly damp sponge.

Patchwork
Tea Cozy

♥

A tea cozy really does keep a pot of tea warm. Even if you've never done patchwork, you'll find this easy to put together, step by step.

Use patches of your poshest scraps or homier fabrics to make a crazy-patch cozy for someone who loves a good cup of tea. The embroidery is optional.

HOW TO MAKE IT

1. Cut the fabric: Enlarge the pattern on page 93. (See How to Enlarge Patterns, page 220.) Draw straight lines (instead of embroidery stitches) to divide the patches, but include the embroidered flowers. Trace the full-size pattern and cut apart each patch. Pin the patches *reversed* to the back of the fabrics. Trace the edges. Add a ¼-inch seam allowance around each piece and cut out the patches.

2. Stitch the patchwork: With the right sides together, stitch the patches together in the order numbered on the pattern, and assemble the large sections A, B, and C. Press the seam allowances to one side. Then stitch sections A, B, and C together.

3. Embroider the front: Wash the muslin and when it is damp-dry, iron it dry. Trace the outline of the patchwork onto the muslin. Cut out the muslin shape and baste the edges to the back of the patchwork to support the embroidery. Place the fabric in the hoop and embroider various stitches in different colors over the seamlines with size 3 pearl cotton, following the pattern for suggested stitches and referring to the embroidery stitch diagrams on page 223. Transfer the roses and leaves from the pattern and embroider their outlines in backstitch with size 5 pearl cotton. Work rosebuds at random with French knots. (**Note:** Be sure to remove the fabric from the hoop when you're not working to prevent stretching.)

4. Cut the back and linings: Trace the finished patchwork edge to cut one back, two muslin linings, and two fleece interlinings. Pin the fleece to the wrong side of the back piece and the patchwork.

5. Assembly: Pin the string at the top of the tassel to the center top of the patchwork front. With the raw edges matching, baste the cording along the sides and top of the front. With the right sides of the back and front together and the cord and tassel sandwiched between them, stitch the edges with a ¼-inch seam allowance, leaving the bottom open. Turn the cozy right side out. With the right sides together, seam the muslin linings, leaving the bottom open. Trim the fleece close to the seamline. Insert the muslin in the cozy cover. Turn in the raw edges at the bottom and slip-stitch the lining in place. From the inside, tack the lining to the top seam to keep it from falling down.

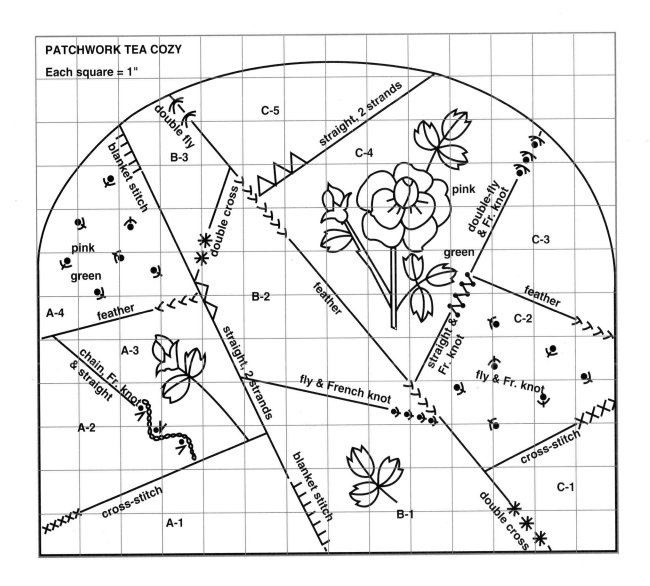

PATCHWORK TEA COZY

Each square = 1"

Heart-of-Roses Pillow

♥

Ribbon roses are glued to a square of white fabric to make the pillow cover. A few roses set the tone, so if you want to make the pillow more economically, you can simply outline the heart with roses instead of filling it.

SIZE

16-inch square

WHAT YOU'LL NEED

◆ 16-inch-square pillow form
◆ two 17-inch squares of white fabric for pillow cover
◆ 2½ yards of 3-inch-wide lace trim
◆ approximately 110 purchased ribbon roses (our pillow has 84 large [¾ inch] and 26 small [⅜ inch] assorted in cream, light pink, wine, and colonial rose)
◆ 1¼ yards each ¼ -inch-wide satin ribbon in cream, wine, light blue, pink, and rose
◆ fabric glue or tacky glue
◆ aluminum foil

- ◆ disappearing fabric marker
- ◆ tracing paper

1. Make the pattern: Trace the heart pattern at right onto folded tracing paper, placing the fold on the broken line of the heart. Cut along the curved edge through both layers. Open the pattern flat.

2. Make the pillow front: Fold the fabric for the pillow front into quarters to find the center and mark it lightly. If using glue, place the fabric square, right side out, on top of a sheet of aluminum foil to prevent the glue from soaking through the fabric. Center the heart pattern and trace it onto the fabric with the fabric marker.

3. Attach the roses: Set about 20 roses aside for the pillow corners. Arrange the remaining roses on the heart, mixing the colors and sizes. Then, removing several roses at a time, brush glue onto the fabric and replace the roses, or alternatively sew them in place. Let the glue dry.

4. Add the lace: Fold ½ inch under at one end of the lace. Starting at the center bottom, pin the lace to the pillow-front fabric with the right sides together. Place the lace so it faces the center, with the header (stitching edge) on the seamline, ½ inch in from the edges. Round each corner with a pleat and turn ½ inch under at the end. Stitch the lace to the seamline and sew the lace ends together.

5. Assemble the pillow cover: With the right sides together, stitch the back to the front, leaving an opening for inserting the pillow form at the bottom. Clip the seam allowance across the corners, then turn the pillow cover right side out.

6. Add the ribbons: Cut two 17-inch lengths of each color ribbon. Stack the ribbons in two groups of each color; tack the ribbons in each group together at one end. Glue the tacked ends between roses at the sides of the heart. Arrange the loose ends in waves toward the lower corners; glue or tack the ends in place. Trim ends diagonally. To make bows, fold back each remaining 11-inch-long ribbon separately to overlap at its center back. Stack the loops and tack the centers together. Glue (or sew) the bow to the top of the heart and attach a rose to the center.

7. Add roses to the corners: Place foil inside the pillow cover. Glue (or sew) small groups of roses near each corner, covering the ribbon ends. Let the glue dry; remove the foil.

8. Finishing: Insert the pillow form. Turn in the raw edges and slip-stitch the opening closed.

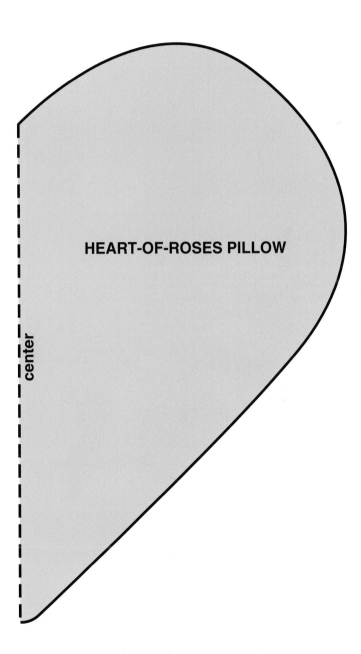

center

HEART-OF-ROSES PILLOW

Lace-Front Pillow

♥

Not all doilies are rectangular. Many have curved, baroque edges. Add interest to these pillows by making them the same shape as the doily. You can make one in an hour.

SIZE

12 x 20 inches or desired size

WHAT YOU'LL NEED

- 12 x 20-inch or another size lace or lace-edged place mat or dresser scarf
- 2 pieces of fabric the same size as the mat for the pillow cover under the lace (to allow for a lace border at least ½ inch wide all around)
- polyester fiberfill stuffing
- invisible thread

HOW TO MAKE IT

1. Stitch the pillow cover: Using your lace mat as a guide, cut front and back from the background fabric, allowing for a lace extension around the edge and including ½-inch seam allowance. If the lace piece has a large solid-fabric center, follow that shape for the pillow. Pin the two fabric pieces together, wrong sides out. Stitch ½ inch in from the edges, leaving an opening for stuffing the pillow. Clip the seam allowances across the corners and on curves. Turn the cover right side out. Press.

2. Stitch the lace mat to the front: Center and pin the place mat right side out over the front so that a lace border extends evenly around the edge. Handsew or topstitch ⅛ inch in from the pillow-cover edge, leaving the same opening. (Place tissue paper over the lace when stitching by machine, if necessary, to prevent snagging.)

3. Finishing: Stuff the pillow. Turn in the raw edges; pin the opening closed. Finish topstitching to close the opening.

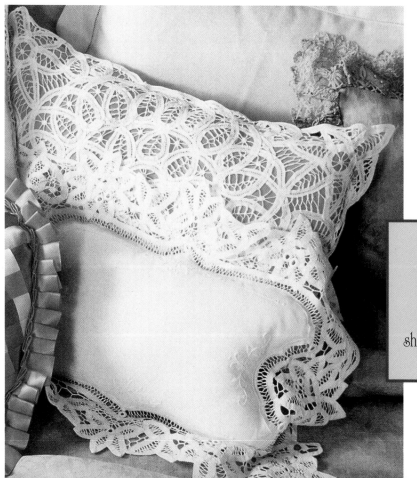

A perfect way to show off old or new laces.

♥

Woven-Ribbon Heart Pillow

It doesn't have to be a heart. The weaving technique for this pillow can be adapted to squares, rectangles, or any shape pillow you like. Create one in bold colors or neutral shades, or with grosgrain ribbon instead of satin, for the living room or den.

SIZE

12 x 13 inches

WHAT YOU'LL NEED

- 15-inch square of fabric for the back
- 15-inch square of muslin or lightweight fabric to line the ribbon front
- double-face satin ribbons: 2¼ yards each of ⅞-inch-wide light pink (A), mint (B), dusty rose (C), and rose (D); 4¼ yards of 1½-inch-wide dusty rose for the ruffle border
- three ¾-inch purchased ribbon roses
- invisible thread for topstitching
- visible thread for basting
- polyester fiberfill stuffing
- masking tape
- fabric glue or tacky glue
- 13-inch square of paper for pattern

HOW TO MAKE IT

1. Outline a heart on muslin: For the pillow shape, draw and cut a pattern for a half heart 6½ x 12 inches on folded paper, following the diagram on page 98. Open the pattern flat and trace it onto the center front of the muslin with a pencil or fabric marker. Place the muslin against a window so you can see through it and trace the outline on the back for the seamline.

2. Lay out the lengthwise ribbons: Note: Pin the ends of the ribbons to the muslin at least ½ inch outside the heart outline, so pins won't interfere with the weaving. To use the ribbon economically, pin it in place, then trim the end straight. Tape the edges of the muslin to your work surface. On the front of the muslin, line up ribbon color D with its right edge along the center of the heart. Pin one end above the heart and the other below the heart. To the right of the center, pin color A. To the left of D, pin C, B, A, D, C, B side by side in order. To the right of A, pin B, C, D, A, B, C. The sides of the outer ribbons should overlap the heart outline.

Made to be admired, this satiny pillow casts a romantic spell.

3. Weave the crosswise ribbons: Weave a color A ribbon across the top of the heart with its upper edge ¼ inch above the outline. Then weave ribbons side by side across the heart, repeating colors A, B, C, D, in sequence.

4. Baste the heart outline: With a needle and visible thread, baste the ribbons to the seamline.

5. Stitch the pillow cover: Pin the pillow-back fabric, wrong side out, over the woven ribbons. Stitch along the basted outline, leaving a 5-inch opening at one side. Trim the seam allowance to ¼ inch. Remove the basting. Turn the pillow cover right side out.

6. Pleat the ribbon for the ruffle border: Starting 2 inches from the end of the 1½-inch-wide ribbon, fold under and pin a ⅝-inch pleat. Then fold forward 1½ inches of ribbon and fold back another pleat (see the pleating diagram, below). Pleat the ribbon until it is long enough to fit around the pillow plus 2 inches to allow the ends to be overlapped 1 inch. Using invisible thread, topstitch ¼ inch from the edge of the ribbon (in the direction of the folds) to secure the pleats.

7. Attach the ruffle: Starting at the center top of the heart, turn under ½ inch at the end of the ruffle. Lap the stitched edge of the ruffle ⅜ inch over the edge of the pillow front. Pin the ruffle around the front of the heart through all thicknesses, pushing the back out of the way at the opening. Overlap the ruffle ends and turn the raw end under. Baste the ruffle in place, ¼ inch from its inner edge (⅛ inch in from the pillow seam) through all layers. Topstitch along the basted line with invisible thread. Remove the basting.

8. Finishing: Stuff the pillow with fiberfill. Turn in the raw edges and slip-stitch the opening closed behind the ruffle. Decorate the center top with three ribbon roses glued over the ruffle seam.

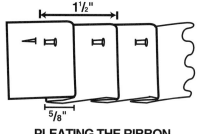

PLEATING THE RIBBON

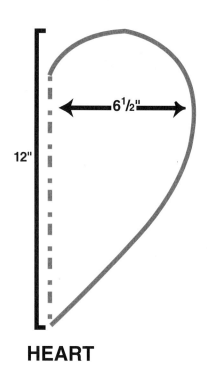

HEART

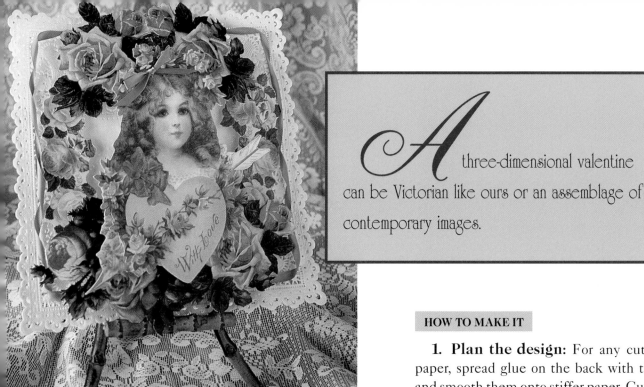

A three-dimensional valentine can be Victorian like ours or an assemblage of contemporary images.

A 3-D Valentine

Start with a valentine, then make 3-D birthday, Christmas, employee-congratulation, or special-occasion cards.

WHAT YOU'LL NEED

◆ 3 or 4 unseparated paper doilies (ours are 12 inches square) or other material for the background
◆ purchased shaped cards or cutouts from postcards or magazines
◆ file cards or stiff paper
◆ craft glue stick
◆ tacky glue
◆ ribbon
◆ ruler
◆ scissors or a crafts knife

HOW TO MAKE IT

1. Plan the design: For any cutouts on thin paper, spread glue on the back with the glue stick and smooth them onto stiffer paper. Cut away excess paper. Arrange the pictures on the doilies or background material. To create the three-dimensional effect, the pictures will be attached to the background on little box-shaped stands of different heights (see the diagram, below). Plan two or three levels for the design, and leave space to attach each stand to the background.

2. Make the stands: From the file cards or heavy paper, cut enough strips ¼ x 1¼ inches to support **the lowest level of pictures;** draw a line across each strip every ¼ inch. Score and fold the cardboard forward on each line. **For the middle level,** cut strips ½ x 2½ inches; draw a line every ½ inch and fold. **For the highest level,** cut strips ½ x 5 inches; draw a line every 1 inch and fold. Glue each stand closed with tacky glue.

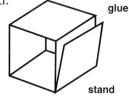

3. Assemble the picture: Glue the pictures to the stands and the stands to the background. Glue twisted ribbon around the edge to the background. Add a bow.

- ◆ **15 x 18-inch piece of 20-count even-weave off-white fabric** (we used Zweigart antique-white Valerie cloth #3256/101)
- ◆ **DMC 6-strand embroidery floss:** 2 skeins of each green and one each of the other colors on the Color Key, page 101
- ◆ **size 24 tapestry needle**
- ◆ **embroidery hoop**

HOW TO MAKE IT

Embroidery: Fold the fabric in quarters to crease the center lines. Open it and baste along the creased lines with contrasting thread. Insert the fabric in the hoop, making sure the weave is straight. Embroider the design in cross-stitch, using four strands of floss and working each stitch over **two** threads on the Valerie cloth (see the cross-stitch diagram, page 101). Each square on the chart represents one stitch or one blank square. No matter where you start, cross the stitches in the same direction throughout to have a smooth surface.

A few cross-stitch basics: Cut the floss into 18-inch lengths and separate the strands to use four together. To start a strand, bring the threaded needle up through the fabric to begin the first stitch, leaving a 1-inch end on the back. Enclose the end in stitches as you work. To fasten off, run the thread under the back of a few stitches and clip. Always end off between sections; thread carried across the back may show through the fabric. Remove the hoop when not working to keep the fabric flat.

To launder: Gently wash the finished piece in cool water and mild detergent (not cold-water soap) if necessary. Rinse until the water runs clear. Roll the embroidery between two towels to blot excess moisture, then lay it flat to dry. Place the sampler facedown over a towel. Top with a pressing cloth and pass the iron lightly over the cloth.

To frame: Tape the embroidery over an acid-free board and insert it in a frame, or have the sampler framed professionally.

A cheerful gift for Valentine's Day, this cross-stitch sampler is sure to become a treasured heirloom as well.

Hearts-and-Flowers Sampler

❤

This charming cross-stitch is done on 20-count fabric, with each stitch covering two threads. But you can just as easily use 11-count Aida cloth and work each stitch over one square. The embroidery will be slightly smaller, approximately 8⅞ x 12¼ inches.

SIZE

Embroidery 9¾ x 13½ inches

DMC Color Key

- Green 911(2sk)
- Green 913(2sk)
- Pale Yellow 677
- Yellow 743
- Orange 721
- Brown 632
- Red 350
- Blue 799
- Pink 956

Cross-stitch over 2 threads

Rose-Blossom Dresser

♥

Decoupage—the art of decorating with cut and pasted papers—is used on this dresser. You glue on the pictures, then add a clear finish to protect the surface and add luster. Things to decoupage are furniture, boxes, wastebaskets, trays, lunch boxes. Possible themes are sports, cars, travel, dance, butterflies, favorite pictures.

WHAT YOU'LL NEED

- an unpainted or old chest of drawers
- roses or floral pictures from decoupage paper or a botanical book or other medium-weight paper
- white primer
- cream-color flat or eggshell-finish latex paint
- Mod Podge matte sealer/glue
- clear satin water-based finish
- brushes for paint and finish
- sharp, pointed scissors
- small flat brush for glue

- fine sandpaper
- a tackcloth (from a hardware store)
- weak adhesive tape
- a plastic drop cloth

HOW TO MAKE IT

1. Paint the dresser: Stand the dresser on the drop cloth and remove the drawers. Sand the wood or old finish lightly along the grain. Dust off the residue with the tackcloth. Following the manufacturer's instructions, apply primer to the chest and drawer fronts. When the primer is dry, brush on at least two coats of paint, letting each coat dry thoroughly.

2. Cut out the pictures: Cut carefully along the edges of the pictures. Move the paper instead of the scissors to cut the details and curves smoothly.

3. Arrange the design: Lay out a border of cutouts on the dresser top and group the flowers between the drawer pulls. Place a few on the dresser sides, holding them in place temporarily with the weak tape. When you like the arrangements, lightly outline the positions with pencil.

4. Glue the pictures in place: Brush Mod Podge on the back of one cutout at a time and smooth it firmly onto the chest from the top down to remove air bubbles. With a slightly damp sponge, wipe off any glue that squeezes out around the edges. Glue on all the pictures and let the glue dry.

5. Finishing: Following the manufacturer's instructions, brush two coats of clear finish over the painted and decoupaged surfaces, letting each coat dry.

Decorate a dresser with cutout pictures of roses as a gift of love on Valentine's Day or anytime.

Heart-Shaped Twig Table

♥

This table would look appropriate almost anywhere you put it—on a porch, in a bedroom, family room, or hall.

SIZE

Top, 16 x 16 inches; height 29 inches

WHAT YOU'LL NEED

- 16-inch square of ¾-inch plywood
- 3 each 1-inch or 1¼-inch-diameter straight birch branches 29 inches long for legs and 18 inches long for rails
- approximately 34 straight ⅜-inch-to-½-inch-diameter branches in lengths up to 18 inches to cover the top
- six 33-inch x ⅜-inch-diameter flexible branches for the edging
- blue-green acrylic paint
- paintbrush
- household scrubber sponge
- nine 2-inch flat-head wood screws
- assorted 1-inch-to-2-inch-long finishing nails
- wood glue
- saber saw
- drill
- protractor
- masking tape

HOW TO MAKE IT

1. Cut the tabletop: Enlarge the heart pattern at right (see How to Enlarge Patterns, page 220).

Draw the outline and mark the three dots for the leg positions on the top of the plywood. Cut out the heart with the saw.

2. Trim the legs: Cut off the top of each leg at a 15-degree angle. If you have no other guide, use the protractor to draw the angle on cardboard and cut it out. Mark the angle on the top of each leg and cut along the line, making each leg the same length. (**Easy alternative:** If you don't want to cut the angles, screw the legs on straight up and down, but install them, evenly spaced, closer to the edge of the heart.)

3. Attach the legs: At each dot on the heart, hold the drill at a 75-degree angle slanting outward and drill a pilot hole for the screw. When the tip pro-

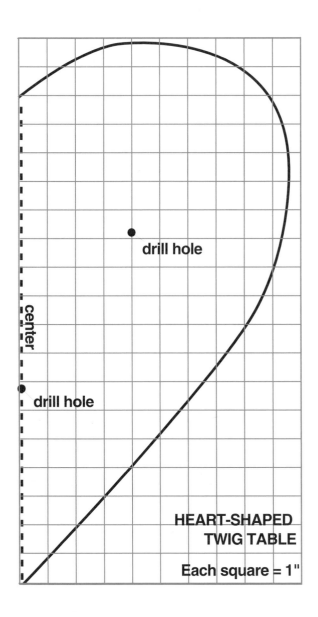

HEART-SHAPED TWIG TABLE

Each square = 1"

trudes, center the top of a leg (pointing outward) under the drill and continue drilling into the leg. Make sure the legs will be evenly spaced, by placing the remaining two and measuring between them before drilling. Trim the bottom of the legs level if necessary.

4. Attach the rails: Mark the inside of each leg 10 inches from the bottom. Following the photograph, tie or tape an 18-inch-long branch to the inside of each leg at the mark and lay the free end across the next rail and against the next leg. Turn the table upside down to drill pilot holes through the rails into the legs and screw or nail the rails in place. Unscrew the top and set the assembled legs aside.

5. Cover the tabletop: Starting at the center, lay two of the thin branches side by side along the center of the heart from the cleft to the point. Tape the branches in place. Lay out the other branches side by side to cover the top. Remove the branches that lie over the screw holes temporarily. Glue and nail the other branches in place, pre-drilling holes for nails to keep the branches from splitting.

6. Trim the edges: Turn the heart over and saw the ends of the branches flush with the edge. With a helper, bend the 33-inch flexible branches to fit against the side of one half of the heart. Starting at the cleft, nail 3 branches side by side along the edge. Trim the ends perpendicular to the heart. Repeat on the other half of the heart.

7. Finishing: Glue and screw the heart to the legs. Glue and nail the reserved tabletop branches in place. Give the table one coat of paint. When the paint has set, rub off some color with the sponge to give the surface a "weathered" appearance and reveal some bark.

All you need are basic woodworking skills and nearby woods to make this whimsical table for a loved one on Valentine's Day.

Paper-Snip
Heart Picture

WHAT YOU'LL NEED

WHAT YOU'LL NEED

- ◆ sheet of gold-colored parchment paper (about 24-pound weight) or similar-weight smooth white paper
- ◆ 5 x 7-inch piece of medium-brown pin-dot fabric
- ◆ small sharp scissors or special scherenschnitte scissors (sold in some crafts stores)
- ◆ a straight pin
- ◆ tracing paper
- ◆ transfer paper
- ◆ tacky glue in a nozzle-tip bottle
- ◆ 5 x 7-inch wooden frame with back
- ◆ 5 x 7-inch white paper, preferably acid free
- ◆ a brass screw hanger for the top, or eyelets and picture wire for the back

For early German and Swiss settlers in Pennsylvania paper was scarce and expensive. Scrap was carefully saved, then cut with decorative edges to line cupboards. Among cut-paper pictures that evolved were commemorative frakturs and the Liebesbrief *(love letter), in which romantic quotations—and occasionally a marriage proposal—were enclosed in eight or more cut-paper hearts.*

SIZE

5 x 7 inches

*P*roduce this picture in the old Pennsylvania Dutch art of Scherenschnitte— scissor-cutting paper. It could start you on a new hobby.

1. Make the pattern: Trace or photocopy the actual-size half pattern, below, including the shaded areas. Do not make a whole pattern, and leave a border of blank paper around the design.

center–place on fold

2. Transfer the pattern to parchment: Fold the parchment in half. Lay it on your work surface, and place the pattern on top with the center line on the fold. Tape the upper and lower edges of the pattern in place. Slip the transfer paper facedown under the pattern. With a pencil, trace over the outlines and shade the areas to be cut. Remove the pattern and transfer papers.

3. Cut the design: Keeping the parchment folded, cut through both layers at the same time, in the following order: With the scissors, snip a hole in the area around the geese and cut away the shaded area. (To cut smooth curves, move the paper instead of the scissors.) Next cut the inner spaces of the border with the scissor tips. Then cut the outer edge from the outside in to form sharp points. Finally, cut away the inside of the hearts and flowers on the fold.

4. Press the picture flat: Open the paper and press the picture between pages of a heavy book for several hours. Remove the picture and poke a hole for each goose's eye with the pin. Then press the design between two sheets of paper with a warm iron. While you have the iron out, press the fabric.

5. To frame the picture: Center and glue the penciled side of the paper to the fabric with small dots of glue. Remove the glass from the frame. Screw the hanger into the center top of the frame, starting the hole with a nail or drill. Place white paper behind the fabric and place the glass and cardboard backing into picture and the frame. Cover the back with brown paper, gluing the edges to the frame.

Tip: You can tint white paper to look like parchment. Wet a teabag under hot tap water until color appears. Dab it all over one side of the paper to create an uneven tint. Let the paper dry, then press it between two sheets of plain paper with a warm iron.

Valentine Quilt

This quilt of simple appliquéd blocks is designed to be personalized and doesn't take too long to make, because it's tied rather than quilted.

Let family members supply the handprints. Use our patterns, or make your own, for the other designs. Things to appliqué on the blocks could include simple drawings of your pet, hobbies, or favorite vacations. The color scheme is up to you.

SIZE

74 x 86 inches

WHAT YOU'LL NEED

◆ cotton or cotton-blend 44-inch-wide print fabrics: 1 yard each maroon (A), pink (B), and patchwork print (C); ½ yard green (D); 2½ yards each ecru (E) and blue (F) for the patchwork squares
◆ 5 yards of off-white muslin for the back
◆ 80 x 90-inch quilt batt
◆ 2 yards of 18-inch-wide paper-backed fusible web to fuse designs to blocks

- a few yards of off-white crochet cotton for tying the quilt
- embroidery needle
- thread to match the fabrics
- lightweight white cardboard for templates
- transfer paper
- sewing machine with zigzagger
- 2-inch glass-head pins
- ruler
- rotary cutter and mat (optional)

HOW TO MAKE IT

1. Pre-shrink the fabrics: Wash, dry, and iron pure cottons, washing dark fabrics separately.

2. Cut the blocks: Cut an 11-inch square of cardboard. Trace the square on the fabric, aligned with the fabric weave, and cut 7 squares of fabric A, 4 of B, 8 of C, 4 of D, and 28 of E. Cut 5 squares from F, leaving enough length in F for the sashes (see Step 8).

3. Cut the templates for the appliqués: Enlarge and trace the scottie, tulip, house, roof and heart patterns, below and next page, or draw designs to fit the blocks within a ½-inch seam allowance. Trace your own or family members' hands and shape simple hand patterns. Cut the patterns from cardboard to use as templates.

4. Cut out the appliqués: Choose the colors for each appliqué and record them by making a rough chart of the layout in the Assembly Photo, page 111, and making notes. Following the web manufacturer's instructions, fuse web to the back of only enough fabric for each appliqué, leaving the paper backing on. Trace the template as many times as required, turning it over to reverse the direction of the shapes. Trace the windows through openings in the house template. Cut out the appliqués.

5. Fuse the appliqués to the blocks: Center appliqués on the front of the E blocks and lightly mark the placement with a pencil or fabric marker. Peel off the paper backing and fuse the shape to the square under a pressing cloth, following the web manufacturer's directions. Fuse the roof and windows to the house before bonding the house to the square. Fuse the tulip leaves to the tulip block first.

6. Stitch the appliqué edges: Before stitching on your quilt, practice zigzag-stitching the appliqué edges with scrap materials, especially the

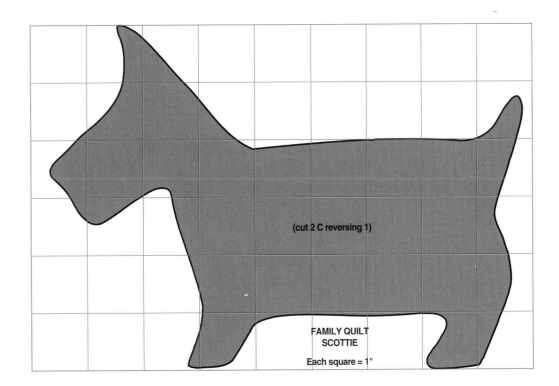

(cut 2 C reversing 1)

FAMILY QUILT
SCOTTIE

Each square = 1"

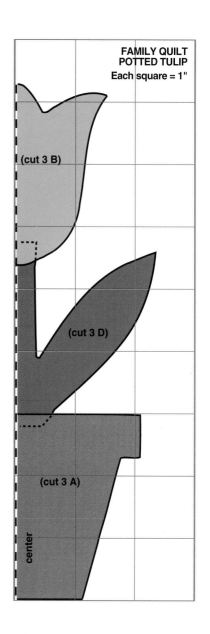

FAMILY QUILT
POTTED TULIP
Each square = 1"

(cut 3 B)

(cut 3 D)

(cut 3 A)

center

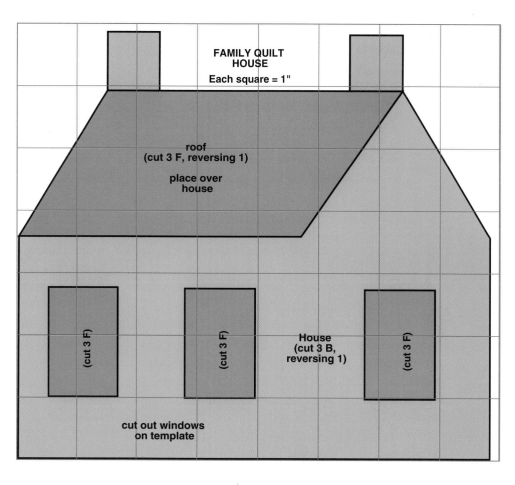

FAMILY QUILT
HOUSE
Each square = 1"

roof
(cut 3 F, reversing 1)

place over
house

(cut 3 F)

(cut 3 F)

House
(cut 3 B,
reversing 1)

(cut 3 F)

cut out windows
on template

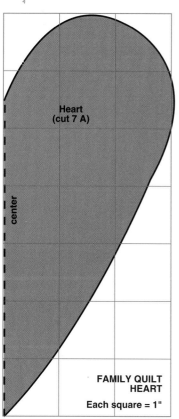

Heart
(cut 7 A)

center

FAMILY QUILT
HEART
Each square = 1"

tight turns of the hands. Then, with matching thread and slightly open zigzag stitches, stitch the edges of the appliqués to the blocks.

7. Assemble the blocks: Stitching note: Pin the pieces together wrong side out and stitch with a ½-inch seam allowance. Press the seam allowances toward the darker fabric. **Center Panel:** Following the assembly photo, page 111, lay out the 35 center blocks. Stitch the five blocks across the two top rows together to form two strips. Stitch the strips together, matching the seams. Continue to stitch and add strips of five blocks as shown.

8. Add the sashes and borders: Side Borders: Starting at the top, stitch the seven blocks of each side border together. **Lower Border:** From fabric F, cut two 3 x 11-inch strips for part of the lower border. Stitch the lower border, as shown. From F, cut and stitch the following strips to the center panel (adjust the length to fit before cutting, if necessary): Stitch one 5 x 51-inch strip to the top of the center panel. Cut two 3 x 75-inch strips; stitch one to each side of the center panel. Stitch one 3 x 55-inch strip to the bottom of the center panel. Cut two 5 x 11-inch strips; stitch one to the top of each side border. Cut two 3 x 11-inch strips; stitch one to the bottom of each side border. Stitch the side borders, then the lower border in place. Press the patchwork, pressing the seam allowances toward the borders.

9. Stitch the back: Cut two 44 x 88-inch lengths of muslin. Stitch them side by side on their long edges. Press the seam open.

10. Baste the batt to the patchwork: Center the patchwork right side up over the batt. Starting at the center, thoroughly baste them together from center to corners and from center to sides to prevent shifting.

11. Assembly: Trim the batt and the back even with the edges of the patchwork. Then pin the back to the patchwork with the right sides together. Stitch the edges, leaving a 20-inch opening in one side. Roll all the edges toward the opening and push them through to turn the quilt right side out. Tuck in the raw edges and slip-stitch the opening closed.

12. Tying: Starting at the center of the quilt and working out, pin the corners of each block through all layers. Thread the embroidery needle with a double strand of crochet cotton. Leaving a 3-inch end on the front, at each pin tack two small stitches (about $3/16$ inch wide) over each other through the quilt and tie a square knot on the front without removing the needle. Trim the thread ends to $3/4$ inch. Repeat at each pin and re-thread the needle as needed. Remove all basting.

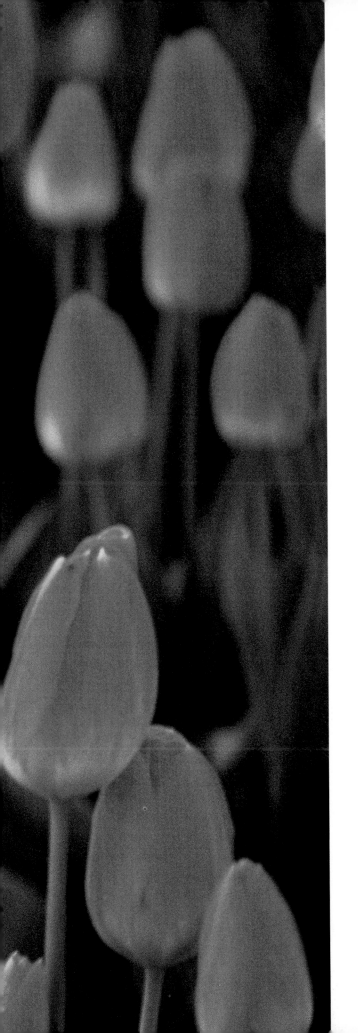

EASTER

Celebrate the season
of renewal

*A*ppliquéd bunnies—an even dozen of the pink-whiskered little thumpers—turn this machine-quilted crib cover into an absolute dream.

Crib Quilt
with Bunnies

This adorable calico quilt could be a gift for a new-born or a wonderful wall hanging in an older child's room. Put the quilt away while the baby is teething and might chew on the pompoms.

SIZE

About 33 x 43 inches

WHAT YOU'LL NEED

- 45-inch-wide cotton fabrics: 3 yards of blue print (B3 for back), 1 yard of solid cream color, ⅜ yard of turquoise (T) and ¼ yard each of 11 pastel prints: 2 more blues (B1 and B2), 2 greens (G1 and G2), orange (O), 2 pinks (P1 and P2), 2 lavenders (L1 and L2), and 2 yellows (Y1 and Y2).
- crib-size (36 x 46-inch) quilt batt
- ¼ yard of paper-backed fusible web
- cream, pink and light-blue thread
- 1 skein size 5 coral pearl cotton (DMC 893)
- embroidery needle for pearl cotton
- 12 each 1-inch and ½-inch white acrylic pompoms for roses and tails
- tea bag for dying pompoms (optional)
- stiff paper or thin white cardboard for bunny template
- water-soluble fabric marker
- ruler
- fabric shears
- rotary cutter and mat to cut the strips (optional)
- ½ yard of muslin for the bodies

HOW TO MAKE IT

1. Preparation: Machine-wash, dry and press the fabrics.

2. Pattern: Trace the bunny pattern, page 116, including the seam of the grass. Cut out the bunny. Trace the pattern onto stiff paper or cardboard and cut it out to make a template. Trace the sky/grass line on both sides.

3. Cutting: Back, binding and batt: Using the marker and ruler, from fabric B3, cut a rectangle 36 x 46 inches for the back. From B3, cut 2¼-inch-wide bias strips for the binding. Stitch the bias strips end to end to make two strips 36 inches and two 46 inches long. Cut a 36 x 46-inch rectangle from the quilt batt. Set all of the pieces aside. **Blocks, sashes, and squares:** Following the assembly photo, page 117, for colors and number of blocks, cut 6 x 8¾-inch skies and 3½ x 8¾-inch grass blocks, cutting along the straight grain of the fabrics. Pin the skies to the grasses in pairs. Cut 2¼ x 8½-inch sash strips to go between the blocks and 2¼-inch squares, as shown in the assembly photo. **Bunnies and inner ears:** Pin cream-color fabric together in two layers to prevent underlying fabric from showing through. Trace six bunnies facing right and six facing left on the cream-color fabric. Pin the layers of each bunny together. Fuse web to the back of the two pink fabrics and cut six inner-ear appliqués from each.

4. Fuse the inner ears: Lay out the bunnies, facing left and right as in the assembly photo. Pin and fuse the pink inner ears in place, alternating fabrics P1 and P2.

5. Assemble the blocks: (Stitching note: To sew seams, pin fabrics with right sides together. Stitch with a ¼-inch seam allowance. Press seam allowances to one side.) Stitch the skies to the grasses. Press the seams toward the grass. Trim the blocks as needed to make them each 8½ inches square with the seams matching.

6. Appliqué the bunnies to the blocks: Pin a bunny to the front of each block, centered ½ inch below the top. With cream-color thread and a ³⁄₁₆-inch-wide satin stitch on your zigzagger, start stitching from the top along the edge of the back ear, then along the face and the front foot. Break the thread, remove the bunny from the machine. Tug on the back thread to pull the front thread to the back;

tie and clip the ends. Starting again at the top of the hind leg, stitch the leg outline, then continue around the back foot and up the bunny's back. Break the thread as needed to change direction, and lap the beginning of new stitching over the end of previous stitching. (See The Art of Appliqué, "To stitch by machine," page 222, for more details.) Stitch around the front ear. With pink thread, stitch around the inner ear. With narrower pink zigzag stitches, embroider the whisker lines. With the embroidery needle and pearl cotton, embroider the eye with a French knot (see Common Embroidery Stitches, page 224). Rinse out any transfer lines and press the blocks.

7. Assemble the top: Following the assembly

photo, lay out the blocks, sashes, and squares faceup. Stitch the lowest row of sashes and squares together. Press the seam allowances open. Stitch the next row of blocks and sashes together. Stitch the two rows together. Press the seam allowances downward. Continue to stitch and add rows until the top is completed.

8. Assemble the layers: Lay out the backing, wrong side up. Spread the batt, then the quilt top, right side out, on top. Baste the layers together along the sash seams.

9. Quilting: Keeping the fabrics smooth, machine-quilt with light-blue thread over the horizontal sash seams, then over the vertical seams. Stitch outside each bunny, close to its edge. Remove the basting.

10. Binding: Trim the batt and the back to ¾ inch larger than the quilt top on each edge. With right sides together and raw edges matching, center and pin the longer bias strips to the sides of the quilt top. Stitch through all thicknesses. Trim the ends of the strips even with the quilt top and bottom. Fold the strips over the edge to the back; turn under ¼ inch on the raw edge and pin the binding to the back. Slip-stitch the edge to the back. Bind the top and bottom edges of the quilt in the same way, tucking in the ends of the binding when you fold it to the back. Slip-stitch the ends closed.

11. Make noses and tails: To tint the pompoms, steep a teabag in hot tap water until the color is dark. Remove the bag and insert the pompoms until they are lightly tinted. Remove the pompoms, rinse them and let them dry on paper towels. With doubled thread, sew on the small pompoms for bunnies' noses and the large ones for tails.

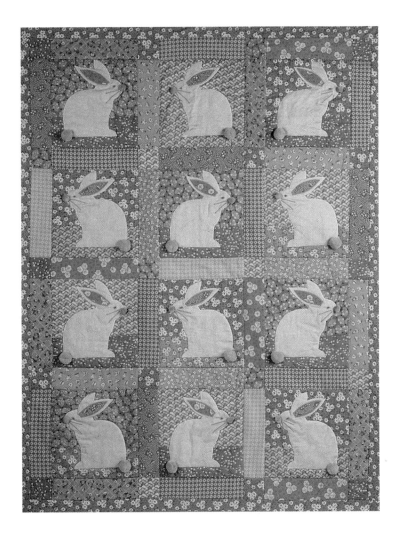

*N*ever had an Easter wreath? This charmer, with its jelly-bean colors and bunny centerpiece, could start a new tradition.

Easter Wreath

This could be a good project for a crafts group or class. Each member can paint an egg or two. If you don't have a toy bunny to put in the center, a chick or duck or nothing at all will do.

- green basket grass
- glue gun
- 3 yards of green string to attach grass
- coated paper plates or palette
- coping saw, saber saw, or jigsaw for cutting out the eggs
- tracing paper
- fine sandpaper
- stuffed bunny (optional)

HOW TO MAKE IT

1. Cut the wooden eggs: Trace the egg, below, on folded tracing paper, placing the fold on the broken line. Cut it out and open it flat for the pattern. Trace 16 eggs onto the wood with a pencil. Cut out the plywood with a saw. Sand the edges smooth.

2. Paint the backgrounds: Following the manufacturer's instructions for the primer and paint, brush primer on the fronts, edges and backs of the eggs. When the primer is dry, paint two eggs each green, yellow and pink with the flat acrylic paint, mixing colors with white to create pastels. Set these aside to dry before decorating. Paint the remaining eggs in assorted pearlized and flat colors.

3. Decorate the eggs: Sponging: Squeeze assorted colors of both types of paint onto your palette. With a torn-off piece of slightly damp sponge (one for each color), dab the paint lightly and evenly onto six of the eggs. Let one color dry to the touch before sponging on another. **Lines:** On the eggs you set aside, lightly pencil simple designs like the flowers and X's shown in the photograph. Then paint the designs in various colors with the tip of the squeeze bottle. (Practice using the paint on scrap paper first.) Let the paint dry.

4. Assemble the wreath: Tie one end of the string around the wreath. Lay basket grass over the wreath and wind the string around the wreath to hold the grass firmly in place. Knot the string ends together and form a hanging loop if necessary. Arrange the eggs on the wreath, overlapped with the decorated ones in the front. When you like the arrangement, set the eggs aside in order and starting with the bottom layer, glue them to the wreath. Place the stuffed bunny or another toy in the center. Attach the toy with string, tape, or the glue gun if it won't hold.

EASTER WREATH

Ducklings

These felt ducklings are easily sewn by hand and are a good project for a group of novice embroiderers. A basketful could be a table centerpiece. Individual ducks could be favors at place settings or the prize at an egg hunt.

SIZE

5 x 5 inches

WHAT YOU'LL NEED (FOR 6 OR 7 DUCKS)

- felt: ⅛ yard or a 4½ x 10-inch piece of white felt and scraps of orange for each duck's bill and feet
- 2 black ¼-inch ball buttons for each duckling
- 2 yards of size 5 pearl cotton in a spring color for each duck (we used blue, green, yellow, purple, and pink)
- black and orange sewing thread
- size 6 embroidery or crewel needle
- polyester fiberfill stuffing
- white glue
- fabric marker or pencil
- tracing paper

HOW TO MAKE THEM

1. Prepare the felt: Cut two 3 x 6-inch pieces of orange felt for each duck. Glue them together to make a double layer for the feet. Set the felt aside to let the glue dry.

2. Cut the pieces: Trace the patterns on page 122, and cut them out. With the marker or pencil, outline the patterns on the back (rougher side) of the felt, turning one duck and wing over to reverse them. Cut out the felt shapes.

3. Sew on the eyes: With black thread, sew a ball button to the outside of each duck for the eyes.

4. Add the wings: Pin a wing to the outside of the back and front pieces. With pearl cotton and the embroidery needle, sew the wings in place with running stitches along the edges and feather lines.

5. Add the feet: With the feet facing forward and slightly overlapped, baste the tops above the dotted pattern line to the wrong side of the duck front between the dots.

Make way for ducklings. Pack these adorable button-eyed felt quackers into a basket, perhaps one you have decorated with green and yellow acrylic paints, and let each Easter visitor adopt one to take home.

6. Sew and stuff: Pin the duck bodies together with the right sides out. Starting at the lower edge and hiding the knot between layers, sew the ducks together ⅛ inch from the edge with pearl cotton and running stitches, pausing at the bottom to stuff. Stuff with the fiberfill, leaving the bill flat, then finish stitching.

7. Bill: Fold the orange bill in half and sew the bottom between the dots closed with orange thread, using whipstitches over the edges. Slip the bill on the duck and sew the inner edge to the head.

Note: See Common Embroidery Stitches on page 223, for the running stitch and whipstitch.

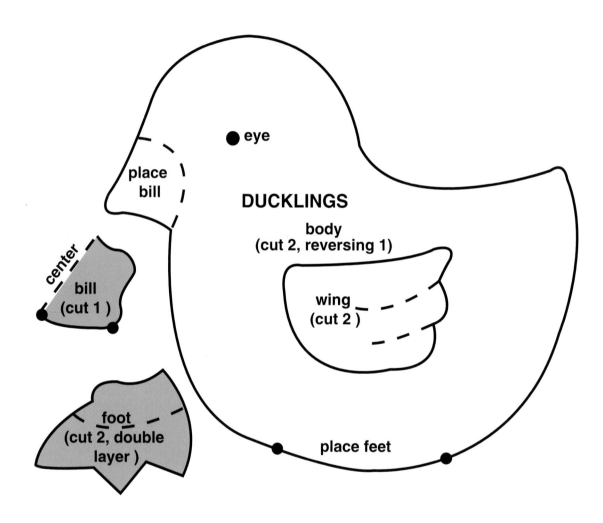

place bill

● eye

DUCKLINGS

body
(cut 2, reversing 1)

center

bill
(cut 1)

wing
(cut 2)

foot
(cut 2, double
layer)

place feet

Garden Eggs

Along with the earliest spring flowers, these pretty eggs could surround the patio at an Easter brunch. They'd also look festive scattered on the lawn for decoration all spring or for an egg hunt.

SIZE

12 inches tall, excluding the stake, or desired size

WHAT YOU'LL NEED (FOR EACH ONE)

- 10 x 12-inch piece of ⅜-inch-thick plywood or other scrap wood
- 8 inches of 1 x 2 or lattice for the stake
- white primer
- acrylic or latex paints in assorted colors
- paintbrushes, including foam brushes of various widths to make stripes
- cotton balls to make dots
- two wood or drywall screws or nails to attach the stake to the egg
- paper for a template
- sandpaper
- saber saw
- wood putty and clear exterior finish (optional)

HOW TO MAKE THEM

1. Make the pattern: Enlarge the egg half-pattern on page 119 on a photocopier to about 12 inches high or whatever size you like. Cut out the pattern. Fold paper for the template in half. Place the pattern on the fold and cut along the edge through both layers. Open the template flat.

2. Cut the wood: Trace the template onto wood with a pencil, then cut the egg from wood with the saber saw. Cut a point at one end of the stake.

Giant wooden cutout eggs have a yummy look lined up along the garden path to celebrate spring.

3. Apply the primer: Fill the edges of the egg with putty if necessary. Sand the edges smooth. Following the manufacturer's instructions, brush primer on all the surfaces and let it dry.

4. Decorate: Paint the background color on all surfaces. Let the paint dry. With foam brushes, you can paint stripes in various colors and widths on the front. Brush the stripes on freehand, or outline them first with masking tape. Use cotton balls to dab on dots. Let the paint dry.

5. Finishing: Center the stake on the back of the egg with the pointed end extending 4 inches below the wider end of the egg. Nail the stake in place or drill holes through the stake into the back for two screws, and screw the stake in place. Screw the stake in place if you haven't nailed it on. Brush on two coats of clear finish, following the manufacturer's instructions.

Mrs. Peter Cottontail

Her clothes are removable, so if you like to design and stitch doll clothes, you could make a whole wardrobe for this bunny.

SIZE

14 inches tall

WHAT YOU'LL NEED

- ½ yard muslin for the body
- ¼ yard each or scraps of blue gingham and print fabrics for the dress

- 1½ yards of ⅞-inch-wide bunny-decorated or other ribbon for the apron trim
- ¼ yard each ⅛-inch-wide hot pink and light blue satin ribbons for the headband streamers
- small rose and blue artifical flowers and pink, blue, and peach ribbon roses
- 1 each ½-inch and 2-inch pink pompoms for tail and nose
- 2 carrot-shaped or other buttons
- extra-fine-point brown (Sharpie) and medium-point pink permanent felt-tip markers
- black permanent felt-tip marker
- polyester fiberfill stuffing
- scrap of quilt batt
- glue gun
- tracing paper
- water-soluble fabric marker (optional)
- removable adhesive tape

HOW TO MAKE IT

1. **Preparation:** Wash the muslin and iron it dry while it's slightly damp.
2. **Make the patterns:** Enlarge the patterns, page 125 (see How to Enlarge Patterns, page 220). Fold and tape the tracing paper over the bunny pat-

She's Mrs. Peter Cottontail, done up in a gingham apron, trimmed with ribbon and a wreath of flowers beneath her ears. Could anything be sweeter? A keeper for sure.

tern, placing the fold on the center line. Trace the half pattern; turn the tracing over and trace the other half. Open the pattern flat. Trace the ear pattern. Darken the lines with the permanent marker.

3. Trace the patterns onto muslin: Cut two 11 x 13-inch blocks of muslin for the body and four 4 x 6-inch blocks for the ears. Tape the muslin for the body front and two ears wrong side out over the patterns. Trace the outlines (stitching lines) with the fabric marker or a pencil. Do not cut out the pieces.

4. Color the face: Turn the traced muslins over and tape them to the patterns, matching the outlines. Practice using the markers on scrap muslin; if the color tends to spread, try to use a lighter touch or allow room for spreading. Then color the face, the toe lines and inner ears using the pattern as a guide for colors.

5. Stitch the ears: Pin a rectangle cut from quilt batt to the wrong side of each blank muslin ear block. With the right sides together, stitch an ear front to each blank ear block, leaving the bottoms open. Trim the seam allowances to ¼ inch. Turn the ears right side out. Press lightly. Create a curve in the ears by folding the ears in half lengthwise, with the pink sides in; stitch ½ inch lengthwise near the fold at the bottom (broken line on pattern). With the right sides together, pin the ears over the bunny front between dots, with the raw ear ends extending ¼ inch beyond the stitching line.

6. Assemble the body: Pin the bunny front to the muslin back block, with the right sides together and ears between the layers. Stitch on the outline, leaving an opening at one side. Trim the seam allowance to ¼ inch. Clip the seam allowance on the curves. Turn the bunny right side out. Stuff firmly. Slip-stitch the opening closed.

7. Make the clothes: Apron bib: Cut a 4-inch square of gingham and fold it in half (the folded edge is the top). Press ¼ inch on the 2-inch sides to one side of the fabric for the front. Cut two 12-inch-long ribbons for the straps. Topstitch one strap along each side of the bib front over the raw pressed edges and flush with the lower and side edges. **Apron skirt:** Cut a 3½ x 8-inch rectangle of gingham. Fold under ¼ inch twice on the short edges and bottom; topstitch ⅛-inch from the edge. To gather the top edge, run rows of long machine stitches ¼ inch and ½ inch

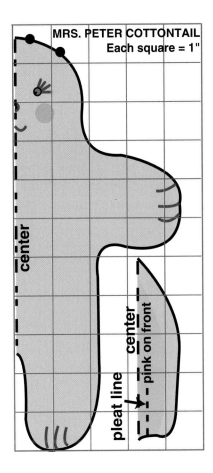

from the raw edge. Gather the edge to the same width as the bib. With the right sides facing you, lap and baste the upper ½ inch of the skirt over the lower edge of the bib. **Dress skirt:** Cut a 4½ x 21-inch rectangle of print fabric. Hem the sides and bottom as for the apron skirt and gather the top, as before, to measure 9½ inches wide.

Assembly: Center and pin the apron over the skirt. Center the remaining ribbon over the raw edges at the waist for the apron's waistband and ties. Stitch the lower edge of the ribbon to the apron and skirt; stitch the upper edge to the bib.

8. Finishing: With the glue gun, attach the small pompom nose and large pompom tail to the rabbit. Glue four 2-inch ribbon strips to the head front below the outside of each ear. Glue flowers to the forehead and around to the back below the ears. Fold one ear forward and glue the fold. Sew a button to each ribbon on the bib. Dress the rabbit and tie the straps and apron in the back. Trim the ribbon ends diagonally.

Bunny Porch Banner

Banners are going up for every occasion, all over the country, street by street. Make your banner the hit of the block.

SIZE

18 x 22 inches

WHAT YOU'LL NEED

- nylon fabric (special nonfading banner or flag material may be available): ¾ yard sky blue; ½ yard each of white and pink; ¼ yard each of medium green, orange, teal, yellow, purple, and magenta
- thread in matching colors
- black thread
- ¾ yard tear-away appliqué backing
- tracing paper
- fabric shears

- small, sharp scissors
- yardstick or T-square
- sewing machine with zigzagger

HOW TO MAKE IT

1. Make the patterns: Enlarge the pattern, below right (see How to Enlarge Patterns, page 220). Trace each appliqué pattern separately, making the grass one piece.

2. Cut the fabrics: Cut the blue background into a 19 x 23-inch rectangle using the yardstick or T-square. Following the pattern for the colors, pin the appliqué patterns to the appropriate colors of appliqué fabrics. Cut the patterns from the fabrics.

3. Appliqué: Following the pattern, pin each piece to the background, matching the raw edges of the grass and the feet to the background edges. Pin the tear-away backing to the back of the blue fabric. Baste the appliqués in place close to their edges. With matching thread, using your sewing-machine zigzagger and $3/16$-inch-wide satin stitch, stitch over the edges. Pull the threads to the back of the banner by tugging on the back thread; tie and clip the ends.

4. Stitch the details: With a narrower satin stitch and black thread, embroider the eyes and the lines on the face, hands and toes.

5. Cut away the backing: With the small scissors, carefully snip away the backing and the blue and green fabrics behind the appliqués.

6. Attach the tabs: Fold under and pin $1/4$ inch twice on the top and bottom of the banner, then on the sides. Cut six 3 x 5-inch strips of the blue material for tabs. Fold each strip in half lengthwise. Stitch the long edges closed with $1/4$-inch seam allowance. Turn the tabs right side out. With the seams centered, iron each tab flat with a cool iron under a pressing cloth. Fold each tab in half and zigzig-stitch the raw edges together. Pin the lower $1/4$ inch of the tabs behind the top hem of the banner, placing one tab at each end and the others evenly spaced about 2 inches apart.

8. Stitch the hems: Topstitch all around banner, securing the hems and the tabs.

BUNNY PORCH BANNER   Each square = 2"

Big Bunny Basket

Fill the basket with Easter grass, decorated eggs, and a few felt ducklings you've made. When Easter is over, the basket will be a useful storage basket for small toys.

WHAT YOU'LL NEED

- 8-inch-high x 9½-inch-diameter or similar-size basket
- fabrics: ⅜ yard of purple gingham and ¼ yard or 8-inch squares each of pink-and-white-striped, turquoise pin-dot, and yellow cotton fabrics
- 5 terry-lined tube socks for the body
- four 12-inch wired chenille stems to support the ears
- two ¼-inch-diameter black ball buttons for eyes
- 1-inch pink, ⅝-inch green and ⅜-inch flat, plastic yellow buttons for the collar decoration
- black 6-strand embroidery floss for the face
- blush makeup for the cheeks
- white thread
- purchased straw hat about 13 inches around crown (from a crafts store)
- acrylic paints in white, purple, and magenta to paint the basket
- scrap of paper-backed fusible web
- polyester fiberfill stuffing
- pinking shears
- glue gun

HOW TO MAKE IT

Note: Use the socks terry side out to give these bunnies their furry texture.

1. Head: Cut a 7-inch-long tube from the toe end of one sock. Stuff it firmly to shape the head and sew the bottom closed. Hand-sew tucks at the bottom to shape it further.

2. Ears: Cut two 10-inch-long tubes from the toe end of socks. To form pointed tips, fold the corners forward and down to meet at the front; hand-sew the sides together. To shape the ears, twist the ends of two chenille stems together to form 20-inch-long strips. Bend each in half to form a V; insert the V into the ears with the folded point first. Flatten the tube and sew the sides of the wires to the sides of the ears from the outside with a few small tacking stitches. Fold the sides of the ears in at the bottom and sew the lower edges closed.

3. Arms: With the knit side out, flatten a sock and stitch two rows, ½ inch apart, down the center. Then cut down the middle between the stitched lines to form two tubes; trim the tubes to 13 inches long, measured from the toe end. Turn the tubes right side out and stuff each one. Turn in the raw edges and sew the open ends together to make one long stuffed tube for the arms.

4. Sleeve: Cut a 10 x 22-inch strip of purple gingham. Fold the strip in half lengthwise, wrong side out. Stitch the long edges closed with a ¼-inch seam allowance. Turn the tube right side out, inserting the terry arm as you turn. Gather, then sew or glue the ends of the sleeve 2½ inches in from the ends of the arm. **Cuff:** Cut two 1¼ x 5-inch strips of striped fabric. Fold under ¼ inch on one long edge and press it. With pinking shears, trim the other edge. With the pinked edge upward, glue a cuff over each end of the sleeves.

5. Collar: Enlarge the collar patterns (see How to Enlarge Patterns, page 220). Fold the yellow fabric in half. Pin the pattern on top and cut around the largest collar line with pinking shears (or pink the edge after cutting). In the same way, cut the next size collar from the turquoise pin-dot fabric. Cut the smallest from the pink-and-white-striped fabric. Stack and glue the collars to the center of the arms.

*I*n the woods, on the porch, in the house, this bunny comes with its own generous basket.

6. Legs: Stitch down the middle of a sock and cut the tubes apart as you did for the arms. Trim the tubes to 9 inches long, measured from the toe end. Turn the tubes right side out and stuff each one. Stitch the open ends closed. Bend 2 inches at the toe end of each leg forward to form the foot. Sew or glue along the inside of the fold to hold the foot in position.

7. Pants: Cut two 7½ x 9-inch rectangles each from the turquoise pin-dot and yellow fabrics for the pants legs. To make a reversible fabric, iron bonding web to the back of the yellow pieces. Peel off the

paper and iron a pin-dot piece, right side out, to the back of each yellow one. Trim one 9-inch edge of each piece with pinking shears. With the yellow side out, seam the 7½-inch edges to form tubes. Turn the tubes to have the turquoise side out; fold up a 1-inch cuff at the pinked edge. Slip the tubes onto the legs; fold and sew the raw ends over the tops of the legs.

8. Bow: Cut a 4 x 25-inch strip of pink-and-white-striped fabric with pinking shears. Tie the strip into a bow and glue it to the front of the hat crown.

9. Basket: Referring to the photograph, paint simple designs on the basket bands with the acrylic paints and let them dry.

10. Embroidery: Glue the hat to the head. Using black thread, embroider a nose using the fly stitch (see Common Embroidery Stitches, page 223). Pull the thread through the head and fasten off at the back or bottom of the head. Pin the button eyes above the nose and sew from one to the other, indenting the fabric as you sew them on to create the bridge of the nose. Apply blush to the cheeks. To make whiskers, run floss from one side to the other behind the nose. Trim the whiskers to 2 inches long on each side of the nose. With black embroidery floss, outline the toes with three long stitches, ½ inch apart over the ends of each foot. Pull the thread through the stuffing to begin each stitch.

11. Assembly: Glue the arms to the basket rim with the open side of the collar facing the basket. Glue the head firmly over the collar. Stack and glue the flat buttons together by size. Glue the buttons to the neck edge of the collar front. Glue the legs to the front of the basket. Glue the hat to the head and the ears to the hat.

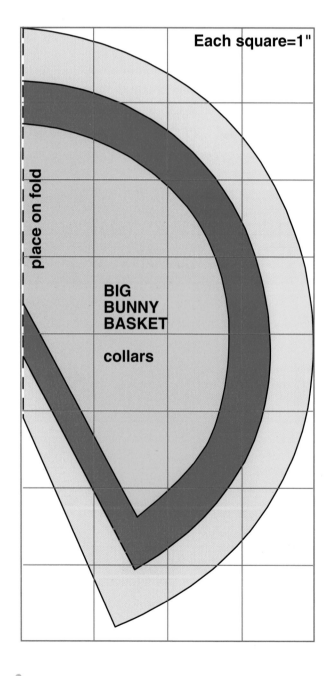

Each square=1"

place on fold

BIG
BUNNY
BASKET

collars

A lasting wreath, it's made with wooden eggs and dried flowers.

Eggs-and-Flowers Wreath

The eggs and dried hydrangea are attached to a vine wreath with hot glue. As a variation, you could use blown, dyed eggs and any pastel dried flowers.

SIZE

About 16 inches

WHAT YOU'LL NEED

- 16-inch-diameter whitewashed twig wreath
- dried and tinted hydrangeas
- ten 2½-inch wooden eggs
- white, blue, green, yellow, and red acrylic paints (use glossy paints or acrylic gloss medium for a shiny finish)
- dimensional paint writers in assorted colors
- synthetic-bristle watercolor brush
- pencil with a new eraser for printing
- 1¼ yards each 1½-inch-wide magenta and lavender wire-edge ribbon
- 7 inches of tie wire
- glue gun
- pans for mixing paints

HOW TO MAKE IT

1. Paint the eggs: In paint pans mix colors with white to make pastels and mix them with a little glossy medium if using nonglossy acrylic paints. Paint two eggs each pale blue, green, yellow, pink, and lavender (mix blue, red, and white for lavender). Let each coat of paint dry. **Add the designs:** With the dimensional paints make small designs of dots, forming flowers or stripes or allover patterns. Paint half of each egg at a time and allow the paint to dry thoroughly before decorating the other half.

2. Assemble the wreath: Lay the wreath on a flat work surface. Arrange and hot glue the hydrangeas to the inner edge and front of the wreath, mixing the colors. Evenly space and glue the wooden eggs among the flowers. **Bow:** Hold the ribbons together. Starting about 6 inches from one end, fold the ribbons back and forth to form four loops, leaving a 6-inch end. Tie wire tightly around the center of the loops and leave ends to tie the bow to the wreath. **(Tip:** Fold the wire over the center of the bow. Hold the wire ends. Then turn the bow to twist the wire.) Tie the bow to a twig at the top of the wreath. Spread out the bow loops. To cut a wedge (dove tail) in the ends of the streamers, fold the ends in half lengthwise; cut diagonally from the outer corner to the fold; open the ribbon flat.

These little honey bunnies may just be more fun to make than to give away. Round up fabric scraps and tiny purchased straw hats and baskets. Then stitch and trim until each has his or her own distinct, slightly dotty personality.

Honey Bunnies

These little egg-shaped bunnies get their distinct personalities from the choice of fabrics and hats. Easy to make, they're a great project for a group. Imagine finding a few sitting on your Easter breakfast table. After Easter, they'll look just as adorable sitting around on shelves. Look in crafts, miniatures, or import stores for small chairs for them to sit on.

SIZE

6 inches tall

WHAT YOU'LL NEED (FOR EACH ONE)

- ¼ yard or scrap fabric for the body
- scraps of black embroidery thread
- four 12-inch wired chenille stems
- polyester fiberfill stuffing
- 1 each ½-inch and 1-inch pompoms
- black dimensional fabric paint or a fine permanent felt-tip marker
- 2½-inch-diameter straw hat, basket, and artificial flowers (available in large crafts stores)

- other trims such as ribbon, ribbon roses, and net for the hat
- basket grass and small wooden eggs, wrapped chocolate eggs, or jelly beans to fill the basket
- a small stone for weight
- masking tape
- glue gun
- graph paper
- tracing paper

HOW TO MAKE IT

1. Make the patterns: Trace the half pattern for the body, at right. On graph paper draw a 1½ x 4½-inch rectangle for the full-size arm pattern. Draw a 1½ x 5-inch rectangle for the full-size ear pattern, rounding off one end.

2. Cut the fabrics: Cut out the patterns and trace them onto folded fabric, placing the broken line of the body pattern on the fold. Cut out two bodies, two arms and four ears.

3. Stitch the darts for the body: With the right sides together, stitch the dart at each lower corner of the body pieces, stitching close to the edge of the fabric.

4. Stitch the arms: Press under ¼ inch on the long edges and one end of each arm strip. Fold the strips in half lengthwise, right side out, and topstitch close to the folded edges. Cut two wired stems ½ inch shorter than the arms and insert one in each arm. Matching the raw edges, pin the arms to the right side of the fabric for the bunny front between the dots.

5. Assemble the body: Pin the back and front together, right sides together with the arms between them. Starting at the bottom, stitch the edges with a ¼-inch seam allowance, leaving an opening for stuffing. Clip into the seam allowance on the curves; turn the body right side out. Stuff firmly, inserting a stone wrapped with tape near the bottom for weight. Turn in the raw edges and slip-stitch the opening closed.

6. Ears: With the right sides together, stitch the four ears in pairs, leaving the straight ends open. Clip the curves; turn the ears right side out. Cut two chenille stems twice the length of each ear. Bend the chenille in half and insert it against the ear seam; trim the ends ½-inch shorter than the ear. Tuck in ½ inch of fabric at the bottom and sew the ear closed.

7. Hat: Glue flowers and other trims to a hat. Glue the ears, ½ inch apart, to the back of the hat crown and bend the tops forward.

8. Face: Make black-dot eyes with the paint or marker. Glue on a small pompom nose. With a needle, run three single strands of embroidery floss, ¼ inch apart, in next to one side of the nose and out at the other side to make whiskers. Trim the whiskers to 1 inch long on each side of the nose.

9. Finishing: Glue a pompom to the back for a tail. Glue the hat to the head. Fill the basket with grass and eggs. Place the basket in the bunny's arms.

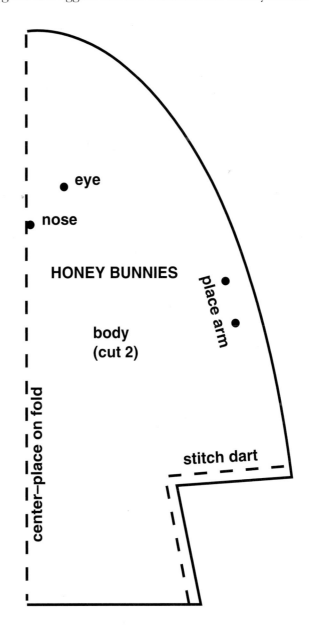

eye

nose

HONEY BUNNIES

place arm

body (cut 2)

center-place on fold

stitch dart

Why not make a bunny wind sock to help track spring breezes? This one has wiggly ears and a winning grin. And while you're at it, get some wood scraps, a saw, and paints to make his favorite food to hang beside him in a tree.

Bouncing Bunny Wind Sock

and Wooden Carrots

Hang this tall fellow from a tree or flagpole a few weeks before the holiday. You don't have to be an expert stitcher or a fine woodworker to make him or the wooden carrots; the stitching is straight and the wood shapes are simple, so go to it.

Wind Sock

SIZE

10 inches in diameter x 44 inches long

WHAT YOU'LL NEED

- medium-weight synthetic lining material or parachute nylon: 1 yard white; ½ yard pink, and ¼ yard each pale green and lilac
- thread in matching colors
- white, pink, purple, and green dimensional fabric paint in squeeze bottles for decorations
- scraps of paper-backed fusible web
- a small amount of polyester fiberfill stuffing
- 5 feet of thin cord to hang the windsock
- 3 yards of heavy picture wire or other wire
- ruler
- fabric shears
- masking tape
- glue gun

Before you begin: Press a scrap of the fabric to find the proper heat setting on your iron.

To stitch seams, place the fabrics right sides together and stitch with a ½-inch seam allowance (included in the patterns). Trim the seam allowance to ¼ inch; clip the curves.

1. Cut the fabrics: Cut two 14 x 15-inch pieces of white fabric for the head. Cut two 15 x 20-inch pieces of pink fabric for the body and two 4 x 23 strips of lilac for the necktie. Enlarge the patterns for the ear, collar, face, legs, and arms on page 136 (see How to Enlarge Patterns, page 220), extending the leg length to 14 inches. Apply fusible web to the back of fabrics for the collar and nose, leaving the paper backing on. Trace the collar and nose on the paper. Cut all of the pattern pieces from the fabrics.

2. Appliqué the face and collar: Peel off the paper backing and place the nose with its top centered 8 inches above a 15-inch edge of one white piece. Fuse the nose in place, following the web manufacturer's directions (use a pressing clothe over the fabric to prevent scorching and add fabric glue afterwards if the layers don't adhere well).

3. Paint the face: Practice using the fabric paint on scrap material. Tape the head front to your work surface. Starting at the top, paint purple eyes, whiskers and mouth. (To make any corrections, the paint can be wiped off with soap and a damp cloth; let the spot dry and cover it with white paint.) Outline the nose with pink paint. When the paint is dry, add a white dot at the center of each eye.

4. Apply the collar: With raw edges matching, center and fuse the collar to the top of the body front. Cover the pointed edges of the collar with a line of green paint and let the paint dry flat.

5. Make the necktie: Stitch the two necktie strips together, leaving 3 inches open for turning the strip right side out. Slip-stitch the opening closed. Turn the necktie right side out and sew the opening closed. Decorate one side of the necktie with free-hand painted designs, if you like. Let the paint dry. Then decorate the other side of the tie.

6. Ears: Stitch the ears together in pairs, leaving the bottoms open. Turn the ears right side out. Measure the entire ear seam and cut the wire to fit. Tape each end of the wire to keep it from poking through the fabric. Insert the wire and pin it against the seam.

Topstitch ¼ inch from the seam to form a casing to hold the wire in place.

7. Arms and legs: Stitch the arms and legs together in pairs, leaving the straight ends open. Clip the seam allowances on the curves; turn the pieces right side out.

8. Assembly: Stitch the face to the top of the body front; stitch the other head piece to the body back. With the right sides together, raw edges matching, baste the top of the arms to the body front 1 inch below the neck seam. With the raw edges matching, baste the legs, centered 3 inches apart, to the lower edge of the front. Stitch the side seams. Trim the seam allowance; turn the body right side out. Fold under ½ inch at the lower edge (including the top of the legs). Topstitch ⅜ inch from the lower edge, securing the legs.

9. Casing: Fold under ½ inch, then ¾ inch at the top of the head for the casing. Stitch ⅝ inch from the edge, leaving a 2-inch opening. Insert wire to form a circle; tape the ends together. Stitch the opening closed.

10. Attach ears: Fold a box pleat inward at the center bottom of each ear. Pin the bottom of the ears, 6 inches apart, behind the top of the head. Topstitch the ears in place.

11. Tail: Trace a large plate on paper to make a circle, slanting the pencil outward to make the circle about 14 inches in diameter. Cut the circle from white fabric. Sew running stitches ¼ inch from the edge and gather the circle. Stuff the circle lightly with polyfill and fasten the opening closed. Sew the tail to the center bottom of the bunny's back.

12. Finishing: Tie a loose knot at the center of the necktie. Glue or sew the knot to the center of the collar. Cut three 20-inch cords for hanging. Knot one end of each. Sew and glue the knotted ends to the ring, placing one along the outside of each ear and a third centered on the back of the bunny's head. Tie the free ends together. Sew the lower, outer edge of the ears to the cords to hold the ears up.

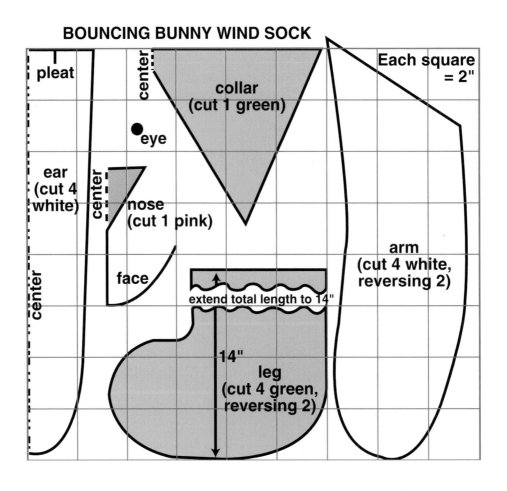

BOUNCING BUNNY WIND SOCK

pleat

center

Each square = 2"

collar (cut 1 green)

● eye

ear (cut 4 white)

center

nose (cut 1 pink)

face

extend total length to 14"

arm (cut 4 white, reversing 2)

14"

leg (cut 4 green, reversing 2)

center

Wooden Carrots

- ◆ 3 x 8-inch piece of ¾-inch-thick pine or other scrap wood for each carrot
- ◆ medium-grade sandpaper
- ◆ white primer
- ◆ green and orange and assorted colors of acrylic paints
- ◆ paintbrush
- ◆ string, ribbon, or fish line for hanging
- ◆ tracing paper
- ◆ saber saw
- ◆ C-clamp or vise for wood
- ◆ drill
- ◆ wood chisel, penknife, or wood file (optional)

HOW TO MAKE THEM

1. Cut the carrots: Trace the carrot pattern at right. Outline the shape on the wood. Clamp the wood to your worktable and cut out the carrot with the saw. (See Making Wooden Cutouts, page 221, for more detailed information.) Clamp the carrot to scrap wood and drill the hole for string or ribbon. Sand the edges and round off the corners. Notch the corners, if you like, at 1½-inch intervals with the chisel, knife, or file.

2. Prime and paint: Following the manufacturer's instructions for the primer and paint, brush primer on the front and back of the carrots. When the primer is dry, paint the leaves green and let them dry to the touch. Then paint the carrots orange or assorted colors. When the paint is thoroughly dry, sand the corners to round the edges and let some wood show if you want a folk-art look.

3. To hang: Insert string, fish line, or ribbon through the hole and tie the ends together to make a loop for hanging.

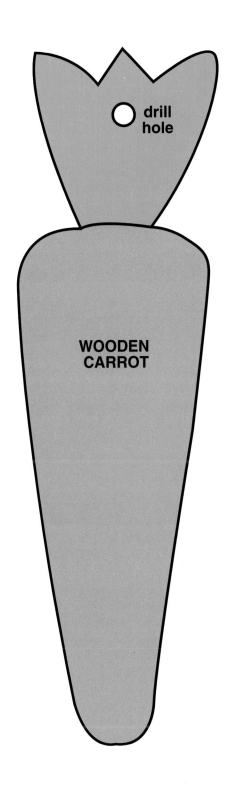

drill hole

WOODEN CARROT

Eggs-traordinary!

Why not have an egg-decorating party? Supply the materials and instructions. Let everyone make his or her own egg-citing creations.

HOW TO MAKE THEM

General Directions: Most of these designs should be used for decoration only, on blown-out eggs you plan to save (see How to Blow Out an Egg, page 142), because some of the materials are not edible and may seep through the shell. Others are perfectly safe to put on hard-cooked eggs you plan to eat, and those are indicated.

To dye blown eggs, keep pushing them down or rotating them in commercial Easter-egg dye. When you apply paints or glues that require drying, decorate half of the egg and prop it up until it is dry to the touch, then decorate the other half. Dyes often include stands for drying, and you can improvise props by placing the eggs on small glasses or candleholders or by inserting thin, stiff wire through the holes in the eggs and standing the wires in a clump of clay.

Torn Paper ↓

WHAT YOU'LL NEED

- ◆ blown, undyed eggs
- ◆ bright-colored felt-tip markers
- ◆ white paper towels
- ◆ white crafts glue
- ◆ acrylic matte varnish (Liquitex)
- ◆ number 2 paintbrush
- ◆ egg dye

HOW TO MAKE THEM

1. With the markers make separate patches of solid color on the paper towels, including a green section.

2. Follow the photographs or create your own designs to decorate the eggs. Tear petal, leaf, and stem shapes from the colored areas. (Daisy petals are not torn paper. Paint them on the egg with varnish as a resist later.)

3. Arrange the papers on an undyed egg and glue them in place. Let the glue dry.

4. With the brush, apply varnish over the papers and around the edges to create white outlines. Wherever the varnish is placed the egg will remain white. Brush on varnish to form the daisy petals. Let the varnish dry. Apply a second coat over the paper.

5. Dye the egg.

*D*aisies, tulips, roses—most of these enchanting Easter designs are flowery. We give you eight different techniques to get your creative juices going. The results will look smashing nestled in purchased grapevine baskets filled with moss, leaves, and sprigs of pussy willow.

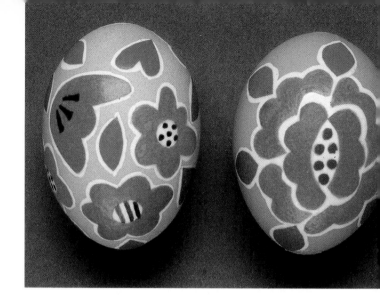

Decoupaged Paper Napkins ↓

(Safe on hard-cooked eggs.)

WHAT YOU'LL NEED

- ◆ undyed hard-cooked or blown eggs
- ◆ paper napkins with printed designs
- ◆ white glue
- ◆ scissors
- ◆ egg dye

HOW TO MAKE THEM

1. Cut away the embossed edges on printed paper napkins, and peel off the decorated layer from the napkin. This will be used to decorate the egg.

2. Thin white glue with a little water, and brush glue onto one side of the egg. Pat a piece of the printed paper, or several small pieces, onto the wet glue with your fingers. Form folds at the edges and snip off excess paper to help it lie flat against the egg. Let the glue dry.

3. Decorate the other half of the egg, matching the design as much as possible.

Cut Paper ↑

- ◆ Use the same materials and method as for the torn-paper designs, on page 138, but cut out the shapes instead of tearing them.

Rubber Stamps ↑

WHAT YOU'LL NEED

- ◆ blown, undyed eggs
- ◆ small (⅝-inch) rubber stamps
- ◆ multicolor ink pad or red, blue, and green ink pads
- ◆ acrylic matte varnish (Liquitex)

- tissue paper
- egg dye

HOW TO MAKE THEM

1. Print the rubber stamps several times on tissue paper. Cut out each shape close to its edge.

2. Brush varnish onto the undyed egg in an allover pattern or in bands, as shown in the photograph, and press the paper cutouts onto the wet varnish.

3. Coat the designs with varnish, including a narrow border around each that will remain white. Let the varnish dry.

4. Dye the egg.

Page Savers ↑

(Safe on hard-cooked eggs.)

WHAT YOU'LL NEED

- hard-cooked or blown, undyed eggs
- circular reinforcement stickers for loose-leaf notebook pages (usually available on paper backing)
- egg dye

HOW TO MAKE THEM

1. Leave the stickers on the paper backing and cut across one row, cutting several stickers in half.

2. Arrange the half circles on the egg in a wavy line. To add full circles, cut through one side of each

ring so you can adjust the shape to fit the curves of the egg. Rub the edges of all the stickers firmly in place.

3. Dye the egg and let it dry. Remove the stickers.

Leaf Prints ↓

WHAT YOU'LL NEED

- blown egg dyed a light color
- small piece of sponge or a paintbrush
- green acrylic paint
- small real or artificial ivy leaf
- tweezers

HOW TO MAKE THEM

Apply green paint to one side of the leaf with the sponge or brush. Press the leaf gently onto the egg with your fingers so that all the parts make contact. Lift the leaf by its stem with tweezers (to avoid get-

ting paint on the back of the leaf or on your hands). Recoat the leaf with paint and make several prints at random on the egg. Let the paint dry.

Markers ↓

(Safe on hard-cooked eggs.)

WHAT YOU'LL NEED

- blown or hard-cooked egg
- felt-tip nontoxic markers
- acrylic gloss varnish, for blown eggs only
- small flat paintbrush

HOW TO MAKE THEM

With the markers, draw lines around the egg in each direction to make a plaid or draw any design you like. To protect the design on hollow eggs, brush on acrylic varnish.

Drawing and Painting ↓

WHAT YOU'LL NEED

- blown, undyed egg
- fine blue permanent felt-tip marker
- pink acrylic paint
- acrylic matte varnish
- fine, round paintbrush
- small dot stickers (optional)

HOW TO MAKE THEM

1. To make the daisy design: Draw circles or stick the dots at random on the egg for the daisy centers, allowing room for petals. With the marker, outline the circular centers. Draw petals freehand around the centers with the marker.

2. Remove the stickers. Paint the centers pink.

3. When the paint has dried, cover the daisies with two coats of acrylic varnish, letting each coat dry.

4. Dye the egg. Peel the varnish off the petals.

How to Blow Out an Egg: Be sure to wash and dry the egg. With a pin gently poke a small hole in the narrow end and a slightly bigger hole in the wide end. Blow through the smaller hole to expel the egg's contents into a bowl (or use a bicycle pump or turkey baster, if you're emptying a lot of eggs at once). Rinse the egg and let the water drain out. Dry it with a paper towel. To dye a blown egg, keep pushing it down or rotate it in the dye bath. You can scramble the expelled eggs right away or use them for other cooking purposes.

Sponge-Printed Eggs

A bowl full of these rich-colored eggs could be a beautiful centerpiece on your Easter table. You just dab colors on a dyed egg with a sponge. Fun for teen-agers, crafts groups, anyone!

WHAT YOU'LL NEED

- blown-out eggs (see How to Blow Out an Egg, page 142)
- egg dyes
- an unused household sponge
- scissors
- paper punch (optional)
- acrylic paints in assorted colors (we used Apple Barrel Gloss Acrylic paints, which have a natural shine)
- coated paper plates or paint pans
- paper towels
- hair dryer (optional)

HOW TO MAKE THEM

1. Dye the eggs: Dye the eggs for the background color, and let them dry completely.

2. Cut the sponges: From a damp sponge, cut a small triangle (about ½ x ½ inch) or punch a dot for each color of paint you're going to use.

3. Print designs: Pour a little paint onto the plate or pan. Dip the slightly damp sponge shape into the paint. Blot the sponge on a paper towel, then press it lightly on the egg. Lift the sponge without smearing the paint. Make several prints of one color, leaving room for others (and room to prop the egg to dry the paint). Dry the paint to the touch with a hair dryer, or prop the egg to dry. Continue to print and dry each color in the same way.

These sponge-printed eggs are as easy to make as they are pretty to look at.

Egg-cellent!

These inventive decorations can easily be done on blown-out eggs to save or hard-cooked eggs to be eaten. The Paper Characters and Bread-Dough Appliqués would be especially fun to make with kids. They can follow our patterns or create their own designs—bunnies and chicks not mandatory.

HOW TO MAKE THEM

General Directions: See How to Blow Out an Egg (page 142). Dye the shells before adding decorations (except for the reverse-print flowers and paper characters). If you're using hard-cooked eggs to eat, use non-toxic paints and nontoxic tacky glue.

Appliqués ↓

Glue on purchased, embroidered appliqués, fabric lace trims, or lace cut from a paper doily. Paper motifs can be colored first with felt-tip markers or paint as shown on the lavender egg at the far left in the basket.

Reverse-Print Flowers ↓

Purchase ¼-inch and ½-inch adhesive, paper coding dots at a stationery store as patterns for the flowers. Create flower centers by pressing small or large dots at random on the shell of an undyed egg, leaving room for petals (refer to the photograph). Cut large dots in half and arrange them around the small centers. Or stick small dots around the large dots to create petals. Make sure the paper edges are firmly pressed down, then dye the eggs and let them dry. Remove the paper dots.

Dried Flowers ↓

Wrap and glue ribbon around the egg; tie the ends in a bow. Glue on small dried or artifical flowers.

*I*t wouldn't be Easter without eggs, and these are some of the most adorable to come down the bunny trail.

Paper Characters ↓

Trace the apron and double bunny-ear patterns on page 148. **Mom (find her in the basket):** Cut the ears from **stiff white paper** and the apron from **colored paper,** extending the ties to fit around the egg. Glue the ears to the top back of the narrow end of an undyed egg. Glue the apron around the middle. **Baby,** below: For baby's bonnet, cut a **cupcake paper** in half to make a semicircle and glue it to the back of the rounder end of an undyed egg. Cut ears from heavy white paper and glue them to the back. Tie ribbon under baby's "chin" in a bow. **Both:** Draw faces with **paint or nontoxic markers.**

Appliquéd Bread-Dough Chick and Bunny ↓

WHAT YOU'LL NEED

◆ A dyed blown-out or hard-cooked egg for each; 1 slice of fresh white bread for each; white glue; small amounts of yellow, orange, and black acrylic paint for chick, pink acrylic paint for bunny's eye; waxed paper; a toothpick and a pointed knife or crafts knife.

HOW TO MAKE THEM

1. Trace and cut out the bunny and chick patterns on page 148.

2. To make the dough, remove the crust and crumble 1 slice of bread into a cup. Add 1 tablespoon of white glue and mix thoroughly.

3. Knead the mixture until it is smooth, adding bread or glue to achieve a claylike consistency. Then knead each color paint into small separate bits of clay, leaving enough dough to make a white bunny.

4 On waxed paper, roll out each color of dough 1/16 inch thick. Trace the pattern outline on the dough with a toothpick and cut out the shapes from appropriate colors with a pointed knife. Cut a chick's wing separately to overlie the body (see blue egg with chick in the basket).

5. Lightly trace the pattern on a dyed egg, if you like. Brush glue on the egg and adhere the dough figure. Glue on the separate parts. With a toothpick, incise any lines (to define legs or head) and let the dough dry.

Ribbon Roses ↓

Glue on store-bought ribbon roses and leaves with tacky glue. For the striped design (center front in the basket), first glue thin ribbons around the egg horizontally and vertically. Make a bow and glue it on separately.

Icing Roses ↓

Glue on purchased icing flowers and leaves (from cake-decorating departments) or make your own if you are a skilled cake decorator.

Painted Dot Flowers ↓

With cotton swabs dab dots of yellow acrylic paint to make centers and use pink for petals to make flowers on a dyed egg. When the paint is dry, dab white highlights on the petals.

Polka Dots ↓

With a paper punch, cut small circles from white paper and glue the dots at random to a dyed egg.

Puff-Paint Designs ↓

Lightly pencil a freehand design on a dyed egg (see the right-hand side of the basket, page 145, for simple floral designs). With puff paint or dimensional paint from a squeeze bottle, go over the lines. Let the paint dry. (Do not apply heat to puff paint.)

Bunny "Balloonist" ↓

WHAT YOU'LL NEED

◆ An undyed, hard-cooked egg, blown-out egg, or plastic-foam egg; a scrap of white felt; pink felt-tip marker; 7 jelly beans; 21-inch strip of thin, stiff, coated wire; two ¾-inch wiggly eyes; two ½-inch white and one ¼-inch pink pompoms; a paper candy cup; tacky glue; wire snips.

HOW TO MAKE IT

1. Trace the single bunny-ear pattern on page 148. Cut out the pattern. Then cut 2 ears from the felt.

2. Color the inner ears with the marker.

3. To make balloons, cut seven 3-inch-long wires and insert the end of each one into a jelly bean. Twist the wire ends together at different lengths to make the bunch of balloons. Trim the ends even.

4. Fold the bottom of the ears in and glue them toward the back of the narrow end of the egg.

5. Glue the egg into the candy cup. Then glue on eyes and a pink pompom nose. Glue the balloons to one side. Glue on pompom hands, placing one over the balloons.

BREAD-DOUGH APPLIQUÉS

ear

BUNNY BALLOONIST

EGG-CELLENT!

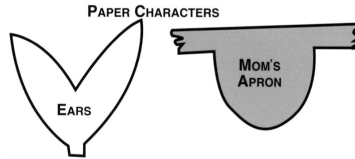

PAPER CHARACTERS

EARS

MOM'S APRON

Quick Chicks

These can be fun gifts for friends, cheery table favors, or soft, fluffy basket stuffers. Easy to glue together, they're a good project for a class to do in one sitting.

SIZE

3 to 4 inches tall

WHAT YOU'LL NEED (FOR EACH ONE)

◆ one 1½-inch and one 2½-inch pompom
◆ scraps of orange felt for the feet and beak
◆ 2 small black beads
◆ tacky glue
◆ tracing paper
◆ scissors

HOW TO MAKE IT

1. Glue the pompoms together: Separate the fibers and glue a small pompom to a large one to make the chick's head and body. Fluff out the sides and cut behind them to suggest downy wings. Trim the bottom flat so it sits.

2. Cut the beak and feet: Trace the patterns for the beak and foot. Cut out and trace one beak and two feet onto felt. Cut from the felt.

3. Attach the beak: Fold the beak in half. Run a little glue along the inside of the fold and pinch the felt to maintain the fold. Then put glue on the outside of the fold and insert the beak between fibers on the head.

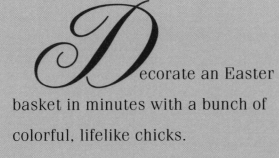

*D*ecorate an Easter basket in minutes with a bunch of colorful, lifelike chicks.

4. Attach the feet: Glue the feet to the bottom so that the tips show in front.

5. Eyes: Glue a bead between fibers at each side of the head, slightly above the beak.

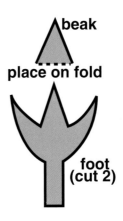

beak

place on fold

foot (cut 2)

*P*lant this enchanting tree on your holiday table. It could become a traditional center-piece to use year after year.

Tabletop Egg Tree

Here's a project for your light-colored fabric scraps. After covering the blown-out or plastic eggs, you hot-glue them to a plastic foam cone, along with sprigs of artificial flowers. Store the egg tree in a pillowcase or a plastic bag to keep it clean when not in use.

SIZE

About 14 inches tall

WHAT YOU'LL NEED

- approximately 34 blown-out eggs (see How to Blow Out an Egg, page 142) or plastic-foam eggs
- 12-inch-high plastic-foam cone for the tree
- 1½ x 6-inch-diameter plastic-foam disk for the base
- scraps of calico and dotted-swiss fabrics to cover the eggs and a 12 x 14-inch piece of dotted swiss to cover the cone
- 2 yards of 1½-inch-wide grosgrain ribbon
- 13 inches of sturdy, bendable wire
- 12½ yards of rickrack (13 inches for each egg)
- big bunch of small artificial flowers for tucking sprigs between the eggs
- crafts glue stick
- low-temperature glue gun
- scrap of thread

HOW TO MAKE IT

1. Cut the fabric: Mark the lengthwise center line around the egg. To create a pattern, lay a piece of extra fabric over one lengthwise half of the egg and trace a shape slightly larger than half of the egg. Fold your fabrics diagonally to find the bias. Pin the pattern lengthwise on the bias and cut through both layers to have two pieces.

2. Cover the egg: With the glue stick, spread glue on the back of one piece of fabric and smooth the fabric onto the egg, making small folds or cuts in the fabric edges to keep it flat. Repeat on the other half of the egg.

3. Trim the eggs with rickrack: Hot-glue rickrack around the egg, covering the fabric edges.

4. Make the tree: Cut off the tip of the cone so one egg can be nestled on top. Wrap fabric around the sides of the cone and trim it to fit, overlapped at the edges. Pin or glue the fabric in place. Hot-glue the cone to the center of the disk. Reinforce the glue by bending wire into a U shape and inserting it through the bottom.

5. Add the eggs: Hot-glue 8 eggs with narrow ends up, side by side around the bottom of the cone. (They may not fit evenly; leave any extra space open at the back.) Glue sprigs of flowers in the spaces between the top of the eggs and at the back. Glue on the next row of eggs, with their bases between the eggs on the previous row. In the same way, glue on rows of flowers and eggs, ending with one egg at the top.

6. Finishing: Hot-glue a strip of ribbon around the side of the disk at the base. Fold the ends of a 12-inch-long ribbon back to its center for a bow loop. Cut a 14-inch ribbon strip for the streamers. Fold the streamers in half around the center of the loop and secure them with thread tied below the bow. Make another bow. Glue the bows to opposite sides of the disk.

Floral Basket

After the holiday is over, line the basket with a napkin to hold bread and rolls at the table. Or fill it with fruit for a picnic.

WHAT YOU'LL NEED

- a wicker basket
- fabric with a large floral print
- blue and pink spray paint, or acrylic paint and a synthetic-bristle paintbrush
- 1 yard of ¼-inch-wide pink grosgrain ribbon to wrap the handle
- 2½ yards of 1½-inch-wide pink-and-green-checked ribbon to tie bows and wrap the handle
- artificial flowers and leaves
- Mod Podge sealer/glue
- 1-inch foam brush
- masking tape
- glue gun

HOW TO MAKE IT

1. Paint the basket: Paint the basket blue, using the bristle brush for acrylic paint. When the paint is dry, paint the top rim pink (cover the rest of the basket with paper if you are spray painting).

2. Apply the fabric flowers: Cut the flowers from the fabric and arrange them on one side of the basket with tape. Mark the placement lightly with a pencil. Remove the flowers. Brush Mod Podge on the back of each flower and replace it smoothly on the basket. Apply Mod Podge over the flowers with the foam brush. Let the glue dry.

3. Wrap the handle: Gluing the ends in place with the glue gun, wind pink ribbon around the basket handle. Then wrap the handle with checked ribbon overlapping the edge of the pink. Glue leaves to the basket rim next to each end of the handle. Tie a bow of checked ribbon around each end of the handle. Glue flowers above the bows.

Ducky Egg

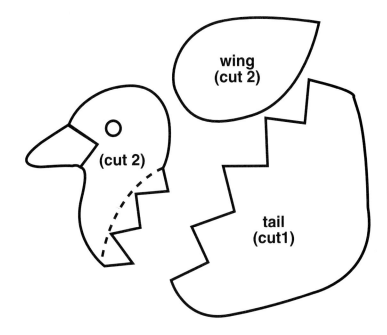

This little duck is a delightful way to decorate an Easter egg, instead of dyeing it. It's safe on a hard-cooked egg, if you can bear to destroy it. Set one on top of a basket or at each place setting at Easter dinner.

WHAT YOU'LL NEED

- undyed, hard-cooked or blown-out egg
- file card or thin white cardboard
- coffee filters dyed with yellow egg dye or yellow paper towels
- 2 small wiggly eyes
- orange felt-tip marker
- white paper towel
- large, flat button for the base
- white tacky glue
- tracing paper
- small paintbrush
- scissors

HOW TO MAKE IT

1. Cut the head, wing, and tail: Trace the patterns, above right. Cut them out and trace two heads, two wings and one tail onto the file card or cardboard. Cut out the pieces. Glue the heads together, leaving the pointed tabs free. When the glue has dried, fold the tabs outward and glue them to the large end of the egg.

2. Tear paper "feathers": Tear the coffee filter or paper towel into strips about ½ inch wide and 1½ inches long. Glue a few strips to the underside of the tail and glue the tail to the egg; hold or tape the tail in place until it adheres.

3. Color the bill: Color a scrap of white paper towel orange with the marker. Fold the scrap and trace the bill with the upper edge on the fold. Cut out and glue the bill to the cardboard head.

4. Glue the feathers to the egg: Starting at the tail end, brush glue onto the egg little by little (thin the glue with water if necessary). Apply the paper strips overlapped so that the torn edges look like down or feathers. Cover the wings with paper and glue them to the sides. Let the glue dry.

5. Finishing: Glue the button to the bottom to keep the duck from rolling. Glue on the eyes and a ribbon bow.

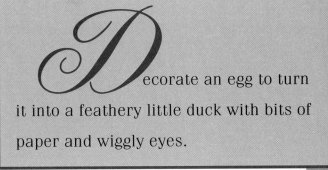

*D*ecorate an egg to turn it into a feathery little duck with bits of paper and wiggly eyes.

Felt Bunnies and Eggs

A great beginner's project for a class of young stitchers to learn hand embroidery, or for you to carry in a plastic bag to stitch while you wait for appointments or watch TV. Cute as they are, the bunnies should not be given to small children, who may pull off and swallow the pompoms or the bead eyes.

- ⅛ yard of white felt
- 9 x 12-inch felt rectangles in assorted spring colors (we used light pink, hot pink, dark pink, lime green, lilac, lavender, light blue, teal, and yellow)
- ¼ yard paper-backed fusible bonding web
- size 5 pearl cotton in pink, peach, yellow, green, lilac, and blue
- embroidery needle for the pearl cotton
- one package each 3-mm, 10-mm, and ¾-inch pink and light blue pompoms
- small amount of polyester fiberfill stuffing
- tracing paper
- thin cardboard or stiff paper
- pinking shears
- tacky glue

*T*uck a few of these adorable baby bunnies and bright felt eggs into baskets, or hide them away with the eggs to double the joy of discovery.

HOW TO MAKE THEM

1. Trace the patterns: Trace the bunny, ear, and egg patterns on page 155. Cut one of each from cardboard or paper to use as templates.

2. Bunny: Trace two bunny bodies on the back (rougher side) of the felt, reversing one, or fold the felt in half and trace one to cut both pieces at once. Cut two bunnies. Cut two ears from white felt for backs and two from light pink felt for fronts. Pin the pink ears over the white ears. Sew the edges of the **ears** together with any color pearl cotton and blanket stitches (see Common Embroidery Stitches, page 223). Pin the **bodies** together, slipping the ears, overlapped, between the layers, with the pink side of the back ear facing you and the white side of the front ear facing you. Starting at the tail end, blanket-stitch the edges of the bunnies together, catching the ears in. Pause about 2 inches from the end. Stuff the bunny lightly, then finish stitching. Place dots of glue on the bunny and glue on a large pompom for the tail and a medium-size one for the nose. Glue a tiny pompom to the eye position on both sides.

3. Egg: Cut two egg shapes from any color felt. Following the web manufacturer's directions, fuse web to the back of assorted colors of felt. Cut stripes or dots with pinking shears or scissors to decorate the eggs. Iron the decorations to the eggs, using a pressing cloth over the felt. Then sew the eggs together with pearl cotton and blanket stitches, stuffing the egg before you finish stitching it together.

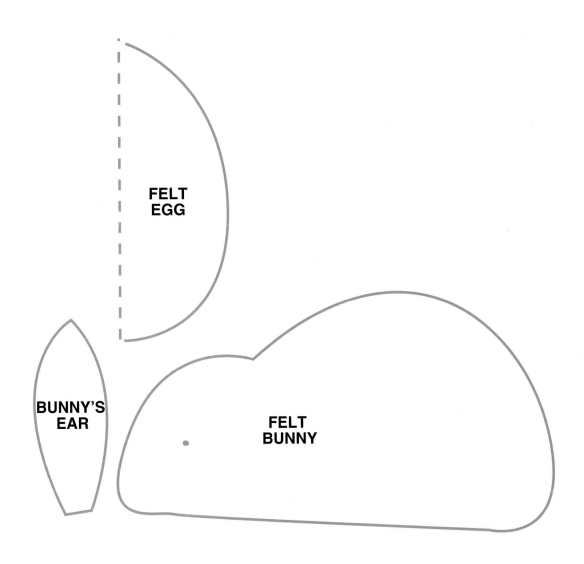

FELT
EGG

BUNNY'S
EAR

FELT
BUNNY

Easter Parade Basket

After stitching up all the stuffed felt bunnies, you could use this basket as the centerpiece for an Easter buffet or a child's birthday party. It could also be filled with small practical gifts for a baby shower. Toddlers may pull off and chew the pompoms or buttons, so give this basket only to children age 3 and older.

WHAT YOU'LL NEED

FOR EACH 6 X 9½-INCH BUNNY:

- ◆ Two 9 x 12-inch rectangles of white felt for the body
- ◆ scrap of pink felt for the nose
- ◆ 1-inch white pompom for the tail
- ◆ ¼-inch pink button for the eye
- ◆ 12 inches of colored rickrack for the bow
- ◆ small artificial flower(s) for the bow
- ◆ crafts glue stick or white glue
- ◆ polyester fiberfill stuffing
- ◆ thin cardboard or stiff paper for templates

FOR THE BASKET:

- ◆ a wicker basket
- ◆ latex or acrylic paint
- ◆ 1½-inch bristle paintbrush
- ◆ glue gun
- ◆ 2 yards of 1½-inch-wide ribbon

HOW TO MAKE IT

1. Cut the bunnies: Trace the bunny patterns, below. If you're cutting more than one bunny, trace the patterns onto cardboard or paper to make templates. Cut out the templates and trace them onto the back of the felt (rougher side) with a pencil or fabric marker, reversing one piece in each pair. Cut out the felt shapes.

2. Assemble the ears: Place the ears together in pairs and trim off one of each pair on the dotted line to leave a single layer at the bottom. Spread the glue stick on the back of the smaller pieces and glue them to the larger ones.

3. Stitch the bodies: Pin the bunnies together, right sides out, and insert the bottom of the ears in the opening on the head. Topstitch ¼ inch from the edge, leaving the bottom open. Stuff the bunny lightly. Sew the opening closed. Trim the edges close to the stitching.

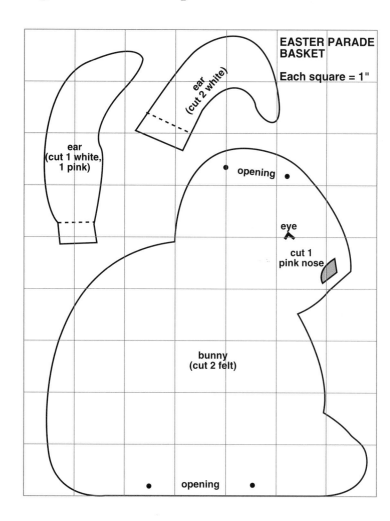

EASTER PARADE BASKET

Each square = 1"

ear (cut 2 white)

ear (cut 1 white, 1 pink)

opening

eye

cut 1 pink nose

bunny (cut 2 felt)

opening

A whole row of bunnies or even one will add charm to an Easter basket. Put an extra one in the basket with the eggs.

4. Finishing: Sew on the button eye. Attach the felt nose with the glue stick. Wrap rickrack around the neck; overlap the ends at the front and sew or glue them in place. Fold another strip of rickrack to form bow loops; tie the center with thread. Sew or hot-glue the bow to the neck and a flower or two to the bow.

5. Basket: Paint the basket. When it's dry, use the glue gun to attach as many bunnies as you like around the outside. Cut two or three 16-inch lengths of ribbon. Fold the ends of each strip to overlap at center back, creating loops. Tie the loops together at the center with another strip of ribbon. Cut the remaining ribbon to make four streamers. Hot-glue one end of each streamer together near the top of the handle. Glue the bow over the glued ends.

*T*his adorable family group will be welcomed on Easter and loved forever. If you can stitch a straight seam, you can make them.

Bunny Family

The realistic, detailed clothes and family grouping make these one of our most popular patterns. Just cut and stitch step by step to complete the set.

SIZES

Mother and father, 19 inches tall; boy and girls, 12 inches tall

WHAT YOU'LL NEED

- 1½ yards of 44-inch-wide muslin for the bodies (⅜ yard for each large bunny, ¼ yard for each small one)
- assorted cotton or cotton-blend fabrics for the clothes
- ¼ yard of the white for the bloomers
- ⅜ yard of blue-and-white print for the father's overalls
- ¼ yard each of blue and white plaid for the shirt; blue solid for the boy's overalls and blue floral for a dress
- ⅜ yard each of pink floral and pink solid for assorted clothes
- 2½ x 2¾-inch scrap of pale green for mother's pocket
- ⅛ yard orange and bright green scraps for the carrots
- matching thread
- gathered eyelet edging: ½ yard of ½-inch-wide and ⅜ yard of ⅜-inch-wide
- flat eyelet edging: ⅞ yard of ¼-inch-wide
- satin ribbons: ¼ yard of ¼-inch-wide light green and ⅝ yard each of ⅛-inch-wide light green and blue
- scrap of paper-backed fusible web
- scrap of medium-weight iron-on interfacing
- ½ yard of ¼-inch-wide elastic
- 6 heart-shaped and 4 round ⅜-inch-diameter buttons
- 10 snaps
- 1 skein each peach and brown 6-strand embroidery floss and embroidery needle
- two 1½-inch and three 1-inch white pom-poms for tails
- 12 ounces of polyester fiberfill stuffing
- pink acrylic paint or felt-tip marker
- small stencil brush (for paint)
- 5-inch-diameter (at opening) straw hat

HOW TO MAKE THEM

1. Patterns: Enlarge the patterns on pages 160 and 162 to scale on a photocopier (see How to Enlarge Patterns, page 220).

2. Cutting: Fold the fabrics to cut two pieces or to cut whole pieces when required. Pin the appropriate patterns to the fold of the fabrics and cut them out along the outline through both thicknesses. (Where small and large pattern pieces are superimposed, cutting directions are the same for both.) Cut and make the bodies before cutting out the clothes. Leave the patterns attached for identification or otherwise mark each piece. Mark the eye and nose placement lightly on the front of one head piece for each bunny.

Stitching note: To sew the seams, pin the pieces with the right sides together and the edges matching. Guide the edge along the ¼-inch mark on your sewing machine (make your own ¼-inch guide with tape on the machine if necessary). Clip into the seam allowances on the curves before turning the pieces right side out.

BUNNIES:

1. Arms and legs: Stitch the pieces together in pairs, leaving the short straight tops open. Turn them right side out and stuff them firmly. Center the leg seams, and topstitch across ¼ inch from the top. On the arms, fold ¼ inch to the inside; form a small tuck at each seam and slip-stitch the tops closed.

2. Body: Stitch the fronts together along the

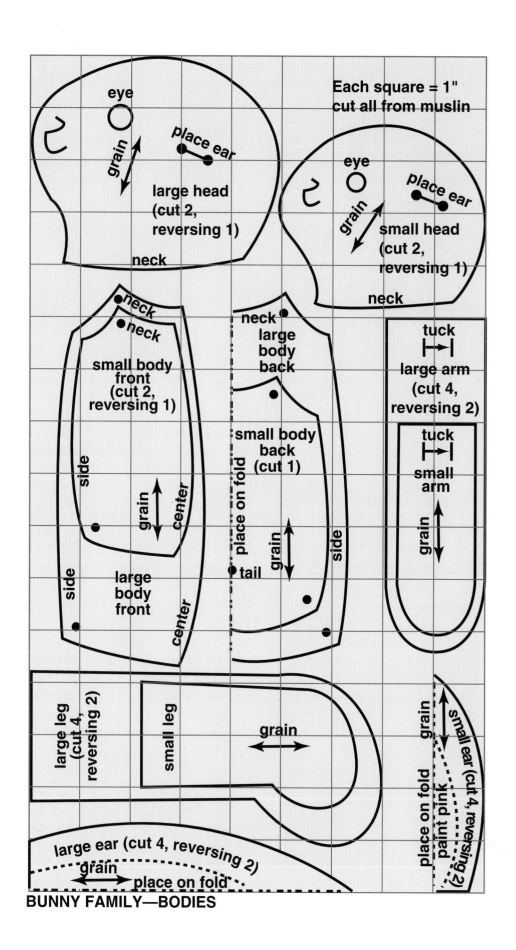

Each square = 1"
cut all from muslin

eye

place ear

large head
(cut 2,
reversing 1)

neck

eye

place ear

small head
(cut 2,
reversing 1)

neck

neck
neck

small body
front
(cut 2,
reversing 1)

neck

large
body
back

tuck

large arm
(cut 4,
reversing 2)

tuck

small
arm

small body
back
(cut 1)

grain

tail

side

center

grain

center

side

side

grain

center

large
body
front

grain

large leg
(cut 4,
reversing 2)

small leg

grain

place on fold   grain

small ear (cut 4, reversing 2)

place on fold   paint pink

large ear (cut 4, reversing 2)

grain   place on fold

BUNNY FAMILY—BODIES

center. Stitch the front to the back between the dots along the shoulders and sides. Turn right side out. With the right sides together and the feet pointing forward (toward the body) and the raw edges matching, stitch the legs to the lower edge of the front. Stuff the body. Turn in the seam allowances at the lower edge and slip-stitch or topstitch the back to the front. Sew the arms to the shoulders.

3. Head: Stitch the head pieces together, leaving the neck edge open. Turn under the neck-edge seam allowance. Knot one end of the thread and hand-sew small running stitches next to the fold. Pull the thread to gather the edge to fit the neckline. Stuff the head firmly. Matching the center front seams, hand-sew the head to the body over the neck edge. Pull out the gathering thread.

4. Ears: If using paint for the inner ear, cut a small stencil from a file folder or stencil material, following the dotted lines on the pattern. With the stencil brush and paint, or with a marker, lightly color two ear fronts pink. Let the paint dry. Iron the interfacing to the wrong side of the painted pieces within the ¼-inch seamlines. Leaving the lower edges open, stitch the ear fronts to the backs. Turn the ears right side out. Tuck in the seam allowance at the lower edges and slip-stitch the edge closed. Fold the ears in half lengthwise, pink side in. Tuck in ¼ inch between layers at the bottom of the fold and sew the folds together at the lower edge. Sew the ears to the head, tacking one side to the head so the ears stand up.

5. Face: Using three strands of peach floss in the embroidery needle and following the steps in stitch diagram, below, satin-stitch the nose. Bring needle up at 1, down at 2 leaving a loop, and proceed in numerical order to stitch the mouth. Fasten off at the center back. With brown floss, satin-stitch the eyes. Lightly paint or use blush makeup to color the cheeks pink.

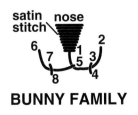

BUNNY FAMILY

1. Cutting: Cut the patterns from the fabrics using the photograph as a guide for colors.

2. Bloomers: Stitch the side seams. Turn ¼ inch under at lower edges and topstitch over the top edge of the flat eyelet. Sew the front seam. Turn under ¼ inch, then ⅜ inch at the top for the casing; topstitch along the first fold. Cut elastic to fit around the bunny's waist. Insert it into the casing with a small safety pin or bodkin, gathering the fabric; tack the ends together. Seam the back, leaving an opening for the tail. Press the seam open and topstitch around the tail opening. Seam the inner legs.

3. Blouses and shirts: Stitch the fronts to the back along the upper sleeve edges. Press ¼ inch at the center opening, to the right side on the fold line to create the facing. Stitch along the neck seamline; clip into the seam allowance and press it to the wrong side. Now press the facing to the wrong side. (*For the blouses only*, stitch the header of the ruffled eyelet behind the neck edge.) Turn under ¼ inch twice on the sleeve ends; topstitch. (*For the blouses only*, cut two pieces of elastic to fit around the arm. Stretching the elastic to the sleeve width, stitch one to the wrong side of each sleeve ½ inch from the lower edge to gather the sleeve.) Stitch the side and sleeve seams. Fold a doubled ¼-inch hem at the lower edge; topstitch the hem in place. Sew snaps at the neck edge and halfway down the center. (**Note:** For the blouses, the opening is at the back. Tie a bow from ¼-inch-wide ribbon for the mother bunny and bows from ⅛-inch-wide ribbon for the girls. Tack the bows to the center-front neck edge.)

4. Jumper: For the mother, cut an 8 x 24-inch skirt, 2½ x 2¾-inch pocket and two 1¾ x 5-inch straps. For the girls, cut a 4 x 17-inch skirt, 1¾ x 2-inch pocket and two 1½ x 4¼-inch straps. With the right sides together, stitch each bodice back to a bodice front along the sides (use one as the lining). With the right sides together, stitch the lining to the bodice along the top. Turn the bodice right side out; press. Topstitch ⅛ inch from each side of the seamline with white thread. Baste the lower edges of the bodice and lining together ½ inch from the edge. Stitch the short edges of the skirt together. On the lower skirt edge, press under ¼ inch, then ¾-inch

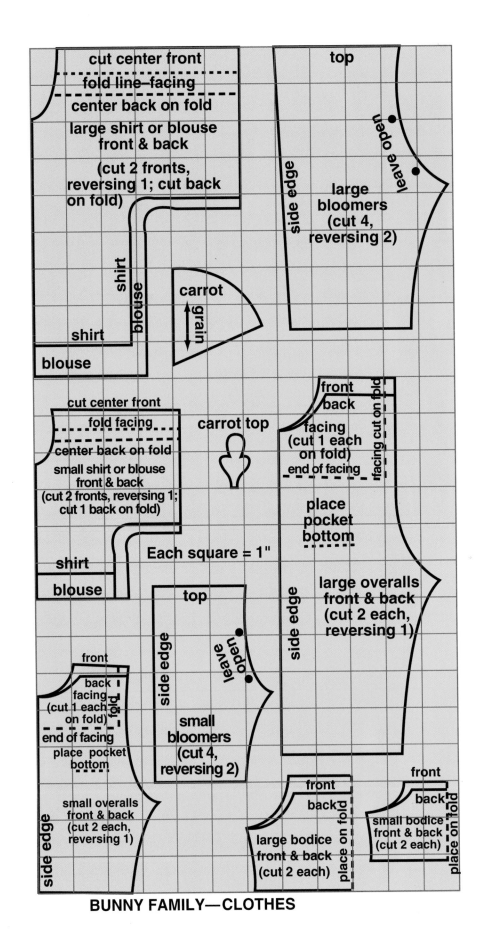

BUNNY FAMILY—CLOTHES

hem on large (½-inch on small) bunnies; topstitch. Make rows of long machine stitches ¼ inch and ½ inch from the raw edge of the skirt. Gather the edge to fit the lower edge of the bodice. With the right sides together, stitch the skirt to the bodice. Press the seam allowance up; topstitch with white along the lower edge of the bodice. **Pocket:** Press under ½ inch on one short edge; topstitch ¼ inch from the edge. Press under ¼ inch on the remaining edges. **Straps:** Fold each strap in half lengthwise, wrong side out. Stitch one short end and the long edge closed; turn right side out. Press. Topstitch the edges with white thread. Make a lengthwise ⅜-inch buttonhole ¼ inch from the finished end of the strap by hand or machine. **Fitting:** Pin ½ inch at the finished ends of the jumper straps to the front. Place the jumper on the bunny and pin the strap ends under the bodice back. Pin the pocket to the left-front skirt 2 inches below the bodice for the mother, 1¼ inches below for the girls. Remove the jumper. Stitch the straps and pocket in place with white thread. Sew the heart buttons to the front of the bodice in the correct position.

5. Overalls: For the father, cut two straps 1¾ x 5 inches and a pocket 2½ x 2¾ inches. For the boy, cut 2 straps 1½ x 4¼ inches, a pocket 1¾ x 2 inches and two patches 1½ inches square. Seam the overall fronts along the center. Make the pocket as for the jumper and stitch it in place. (For the small bunny, press ¼ inch under on the patch edges; topstitch the patches slightly slanted to the front of the legs 1 inch below the pocket.) Stitch the backs together, marking and leaving an opening for the tail; press the seam open. Topstitch around the opening. Seam the sides of the overalls and the facings. Stitch the facings to the upper edge; clip the curves and turn. Press. Topstitch the edge with white thread. Topstitch a doubled ¼-inch hem on the bottom of the legs. Seam the legs. Attach straps and round buttons as for the jumper.

6. Neckerchiefs: Cut a 9½-inch square for the father's neckerchief, a 7-inch square for the son's. Fold each in half diagonally and cut to use one triangle. Turn under ¼ inch all around; topstitch. Tie the neckerchiefs around the bunnies' necks.

7. Carrot (for large bunnies): Fuse two layers of green fabric together with web; cut the carrot top. Cut the carrot from orange fabric and stitch the side closed. Turn the carrot right side out. Stuff. Gather the top of the carrot. Turn in the seam allowance and insert the green top; sew the top closed. Place the carrot in the pocket.

8. Hat: Cut holes for ears in the straw hat brim and place the hat on the father bunny's head.

Bunny-House Pillow

SIZE

12-inch square, plus the ruffle

This pillow looks complex, but it can even be made in quantity for a bazaar if you give each person a separate task: cutting fabric, appliquéing, pillow assembly, bunny making, and dressmaking.

WHAT YOU'LL NEED

FOR THE PILLOW AND BUNNIES:
- ◆ tracing paper
- ◆ paper for pattern
- ◆ masking tape or clear tape
- ◆ thread to match fabrics
- ◆ pinking shears
- ◆ polyester fiberfill stuffing

What little girl wouldn't love this magical house pillow with four little rabbits to pop in and out of the pocket windows?

FOR THE PILLOW ONLY:
- cotton or cotton-blend fabrics
- ⅔ yard of blue polished cotton
- ⅓ yard of raspberry and pink printed cotton
- ⅛ yard each of yellow and pink polished cotton, soft green calico and dark red plaid
- 1-inch square of red cotton
- 1 yard of paper-backed fusible web
- 1 yard ¼-inch-wide yellow satin ribbon
- 3½ yards of 2½-inch-wide flat ivory (or white) eyelet trim
- 33 small purchased ribbon roses
- tacky glue
- small (7-mm) black ball button
- ruler
- sewing machine with zigzagger
- optional: rotary cutter, mat, and see-through ruler

FOR THE FOUR BUNNIES:
- ½ yard of muslin for the bodies
- ⅛ yard each tiny blue and orchid gingham, yellow print and bright pink solid cotton for clothes
- 2 yards of ¼-inch-wide ivory lace trim
- ½ yard each ¼-inch-wide raspberry and blue satin ribbon
- 2 purchased ribbon roses
- four ⅜-inch buttons: raspberry heart, white heart, blue flat round, pink flat round
- permanent fine-point felt-tip markers: black, brown (Sharpie Ultra fine), pink, and blue
- disappearing fabric marker

Stitching note: To stitch seams, pin pieces with the right sides together and stitch with a ¼-inch seam allowance unless otherwise indicated.

1. Patterns: Enlarge the house pattern, below (see How to Enlarge Patterns, page 220). Trace each pocket (window) and each appliqué separately from the full-size pattern, following the broken lines for the underlapped edges of the house and chimney base.

2. Cutting: Pillow cover: Cut two 13-inch squares of blue fabric. **Ruffle:** Cut three 3 x 36-inch strips across the blue fabric. **Pockets (windows):** Adding a ¼-inch seam allowance all around, cut 2 pink pieces (front and lining) for each window/

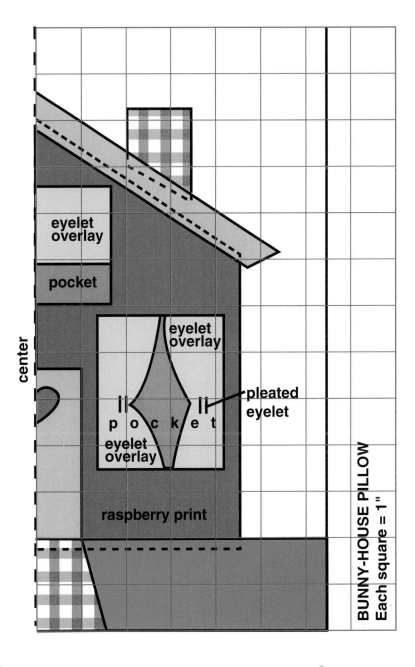

BUNNY-HOUSE PILLOW
Each square = 1"

pocket. **House:** Following the web manufacturer's instructions and the colors on the pattern, iron the fusible web to the backs of the fabrics for the appliqué, leaving the paper backing on. Trace the appliqué patterns on the back of appropriate colors and cut them out. **Note:** Cut only one chimney. Remove the paper backing.

3. Appliqué: Following the pattern, assemble the appliqués on the pillow-front fabric and iron

them in place, again following the web manufacturer's directions. With matching thread, satin-stitch over the edge of each piece with your sewing-machine zigzagger, making the stitches a scant ⅛ inch wide (see The Art of Appliqué, "To stitch by machine," page 222, for more details). Pull the threads to the back by tugging on the back thread; tie and clip the ends.

4. Pockets: Pin the eyelet for the curtains over the pocket fronts as indicated on the pattern; trim the eyelet edges to match the pocket. Pinch and top-stitch "pleats" for the tiebacks in the lower-window curtains. With the right sides together, stitch the pockets to the pocket linings, leaving an opening at the bottom for turning. Clip the seam allowance across the corners; turn the pocket right side out. Tuck in the raw edges at the opening; press. Pin the pockets to the house and topstitch close to their sides and lower edges.

5. Ruffle: Stitch the blue strips together end to end to form a circle. Press the seams open. Press one edge under ¼ inch twice; topstitch ⅛ inch from the edge. Stitch eyelet into a circle the same size. Pin the eyelet circle over the blue one with the raw edges matching. Make rows of long machine stitches ¼ inch and ½ inch from the raw edges for gathering, or see the tip on the next page.

6. Attach the ruffle to the front: Fold the ruffle-circle in half twice and mark each fold with a pin to mark the circle in four equal parts. Open the circle flat. With the right sides together and the raw edges matching, pin the ruffle at the markers to the

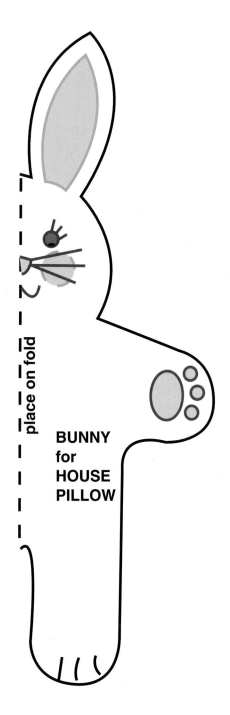

place on fold

**BUNNY
for
HOUSE
PILLOW**

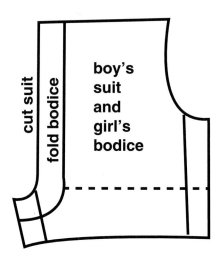

cut suit

fold bodice

**boy's
suit
and
girl's
bodice**

center of the pillow-front edges. Gather the ruffle evenly to fit around the pillow front, pushing a little extra fullness into the corners. Pin, then baste the ruffle in place ½ inch from the raw edge.

7. Assembly: With the right sides together, pin the back to the front. Starting at the bottom, stitch along the basting, leaving 6 inches open at the bottom. Clip across the corners of the seam allowance. Turn the pillow right side out. Press. Stuff firmly. Slip-stitch the opening closed.

8. Finishing: Sew the button to the center of the left-hand side of the door as a doorknob. Tie four 1¼-inch-wide bows of yellow ribbon, and glue or tack one each over the curtain pleats. Glue six roses below each lower window. Glue the roses below the upper window and below the house at the grass line.

HOW TO MAKE THE BUNNIES

1. Patterns: Trace the half bunny, page 166, onto folded tracing paper, placing the fold on the broken line. Turn the paper over and trace the other half. Open the pattern flat and darken the lines with a black marker. Trace the clothes pattern, page 166.

2. Coloring: Note: The exact bunny shape isn't cut until after you've stitched. Cut two 6 x 8-inch muslin rectangles for each bunny. Tape one muslin piece, right side out, over the pattern. With markers, color the pink and blue areas. Outline the details in brown.

3. Stitching: Turn the muslin over and align the details with the pattern. Now trace the bunny outline with the disappearing marker. Remove the tape. Pin the two muslin rectangles with right sides together. Stitch along the bunny outline, leaving a 1¼-inch opening on the outside of one leg. With pinking shears, trim the fabric to ¼ inch from the

seam. Clip the corners. Turn the bunny right side out. Stuff the ears. Topstitch across the bottom of the ears. Stuff the rest of the bunny; slip-stitch the opening closed.

4. Boys' suits (make 2): Following the photograph for colors, cut four pattern pieces (reversing two) from fabric for each suit. Stitch the center back and front seams. Stitch the side seams. Press the seams open. Zigzag-stitch along the raw edges of the suit top, armholes and lower leg edge. **Rickrack:** Pin rickrack across the top and leg edges; stitch through the center of the rickrack. Starting at the back, stitch rickrack around each armhole and cut off the ends 2 inches above the front for shoulder straps. **Finishing:** Stitch the leg seam. Sew a button to the front chest. Slip the pants on the bunny and tack the shoulder straps to the back corners; trim the ends.

5. Girls' dresses (make 2): For each dress, fold the fabric in half and cut two pattern pieces for the bodice with the center on the fold and the bottom on the broken line. Cut a 2 x 12-inch fabric strip for the skirt. Zigzag-stitch along the edges of the skirt hem, armholes and bodice top. Stitch the bodice side seams; press the seam allowances open. **Lace:** Press the stitching on the zigzagged edges to the wrong side. Lap and pin the hem edge over the stitching edge of the lace; topstitch along the hem edge. Stitch lace to the bodice top, then to the armholes, extending the front ends to make 2-inch-long shoulder straps as for the suits. **Finishing:** Stitch the skirt together at the short ends to form a circle. Gather the raw edge to fit the bodice. Stitch the skirt to the bodice on the broken line with a ½-inch seam allowance. Decorate the dress with a heart button on the front and a bow at the waist. Glue or tack a bow topped with a rose below the girl's ear.

Tip: Since long sewing threads may break when gathered, try zigzagging large stitches over string or carpet thread laid on the fabric. Don't catch the thread in the stitches. Slide the fabric along the thread to gather. Secure the ends with straight pins before stitching.

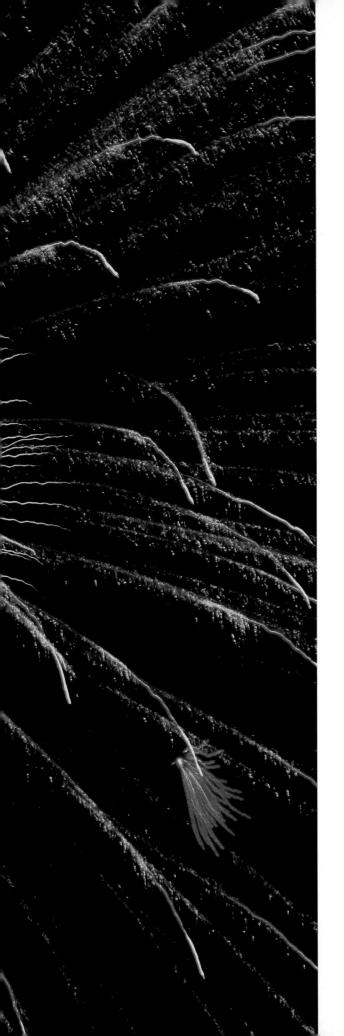

Independence Day

How lucky we are

Stars-and-Stripes Banner

On the front door, a porch, or the wall behind a Fourth-of-July buffet, this flag will set the stage for celebrations.

SIZE

25 x 34 inches

WHAT YOU'LL NEED

- ◆ felt: 1 yard red, 12-inch square blue, ½ yard white or five 9 x 12-inch pieces of sticky-back white press-on felt
- ◆ 26 x 36-inch piece of stiff cardboard or illustration board for back
- ◆ 1 yard of gold cord about ½ inch thick
- ◆ gold tassel (optional)
- ◆ scrap of tracing paper
- ◆ file card or small piece of thin cardboard
- ◆ crafts knife
- ◆ spray adhesive
- ◆ white glue

- glue gun
- soft, dark pencil
- white chalk or white pencil
- 2 cloth hook-and-eyelet picture hangers

HOW TO MAKE IT

1. **Make the pattern:** Enlarge the flag pattern below (see How to Enlarge Patterns, page 220). Cut out the pattern on the flag outline. Trace the star.

2. **Cut the background:** Trace the flag outline onto the cardboard. Holding the craft knife against a ruler to guide straight lines, score the board several times to cut through.

3. **Apply the red felt:** Trace the cardboard flag onto the red felt and cut the flag from the felt. Spray adhesive on the cardboard, then position and smooth the felt in place. **Note:** Be sure to work in a well-ventilated place when using spray adhesive.

4. **Add the blue field:** Cut the blue field from the pattern. Pin it to the blue felt and cut it out. Spray adhesive on the back of the blue felt, and smooth it in place on the flag on top of the red felt.

5. **White stripes:** Pin the pattern to white felt and cut out the white stripes. Adhere the stripes evenly spaced to the red felt with white glue or spray adhesive or according to the instructions for the sticky-back felt. (If the sticky-back felt requires ironing, as directed by the manufacturer, use a pressing cloth and a low to medium heat setting, because the spray adhesive is flammable.)

6. **Stars:** Trace the star pattern onto thin cardboard to use as a template and cut out the template. Trace 26 stars onto white felt and cut them out. Perforate the holes on the blue field pattern with the tip of a pencil. Lay the pattern on the blue field and mark it through the holes with white chalk or pencil. Use white glue or the sticky-back to adhere stars over the dots.

7. **Finishing:** Tie a knot at the top of the gold cord and attach the cord along the flag's left edge with the glue gun. Knot the cord at the bottom of the flag and unravel excess cord to let 5-inch ends hang, or tie on a tassel. Hot-glue the eyelet hangers to the back about 4 inches in from the upper corners.

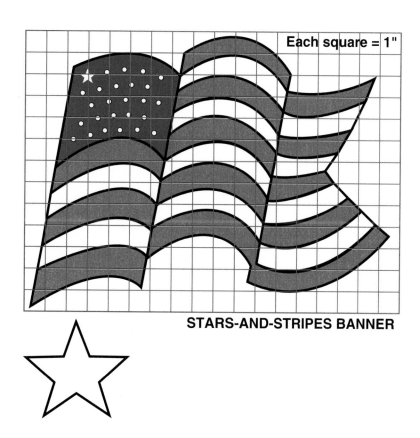

Each square = 1"

STARS-AND-STRIPES BANNER

Uncle Sam Whirligig

★

All the wooden pieces, except the circular hat brim, are cut straight. The metal flags are easily made. Omit the wooden stars if you like.

SIZE

20 inches tall

WHAT YOU'LL NEED

- ¾-inch pine or other wood: 5½-inch square for base, 3-inch-diameter circle for hat brim, 1¼-inch square for beard, and three 4-inch squares for stars
- 21-inch strip of wood 1 x 1 for legs
- 3½-inch square of wood 2 x 4 for body
- 10-inch x ⅞-inch-diameter dowel for arms and hat crown
- 18-inch x ¼-inch-diameter dowel for peg joints and arm axle
- 3 x 9-inch metal roof flashing for flags
- red, yellow, blue, black, and white acrylic paints
- 1-inch flat and small round paintbrushes
- three 18-inch lengths of 16-gauge wire (or wire hangers)
- household cement
- wood glue
- 2 each 1½-inch finishing nails and flat-head wood screws
- thin nail
- pliers
- metal and wire cutters
- drill with ¹⁄₁₆- and ¼-inch bits and a ⁵⁄₁₆- or ⅜-inch spade bit or regular bit with extension
- 3 x 4-inch piece of transfer paper

- medium-grade sandpaper
- polyurethane or exterior clear finish
- saber saw
- worktable with vise
- tracing paper

Note: Glue metal to metal or to wood with household cement; glue wood to wood with wood glue. **To make peg joints:** The legs and head are joined to the body with pegs. To make a peg, cut a 2-inch length from the ¼-inch dowel. Placing wood in the vise, drill a 1-inch-deep x ¼-inch-diameter hole centered in the edge of one piece to be joined. Insert the dowel. Mark the edge of the other piece precisely for a matching hole; drill the hole. Glue opposite ends of the dowel into the holes.

HOW TO MAKE IT

1. **Cutting:** Following the Assembly Diagram on page 174, cut the pieces from the wood. Sand the cut edges.

2. **Stars:** Draw 3 stars about 3 inches wide freehand (or trace a star from page 178) on ¾-inch-thick wood and cut them out. Cut 5-, 7- and 9-inch lengths of heavy wire. With the ¹⁄₁₆-inch bit (or appropriate size for your wire), drill a 1-inch-deep hole for the wire in the bottom of each star. Glue the wire into the holes. Set the stars aside.

3. **Arms:** Drill a ⁵⁄₁₆- or ⅜-inch-diameter hole from side to side through the body, centered ⅝ inch below the top for the arm-axle dowel. Drill a 1-inch-deep ¼-inch-diamater hole centered in one end (shoulder end) of each arm dowel to attach arms to the axle later.

4. **Legs and head:** Center the legs on the bottom of the body block and attach with dowel pegs. Peg the head to the center of the top edge of the body with the front surfaces matching. Glue and nail the beard to the chin.

5. **Hat:** Glue and nail the dowel that forms the crown of the hat to the center of the circular brim from the underside, leaving about ¼ inch at the top of the nail exposed. Nip off the nailhead with the wire cutters. Center and glue the hat to the head, tapping in the exposed end of the nail.

6. **Base:** Trace the leg positions on the center of

*E*very little
breeze turns this Uncle Sam
into a two-fisted flag-waver.

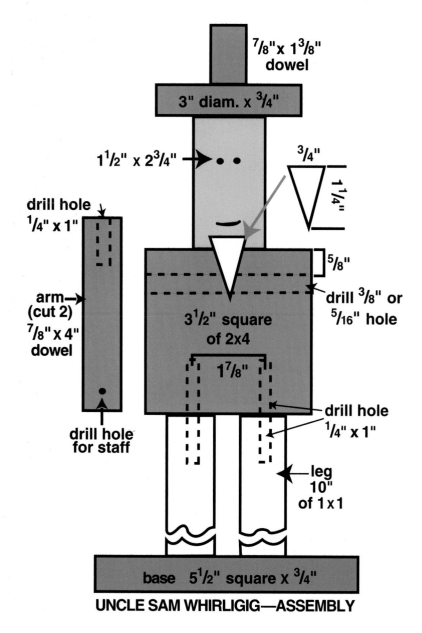

7/8" x 1 3/8" dowel

3" diam. x 3/4"

1 1/2" x 2 3/4" →

3/4"

1 1/4"

drill hole 1/4" x 1"

arm—(cut 2) 7/8" x 4" dowel

5/8"

drill 3/8" or 5/16" hole

3 1/2" square of 2x4

1 7/8"

drill hole 1/4" x 1"

drill hole for staff

leg 10" of 1 x 1

base 5 1/2" square x 3/4"

UNCLE SAM WHIRLIGIG—ASSEMBLY

the bottom of the base. Drill pilot holes for screws through the base into the legs. Glue the legs to the top of the base over the holes and screw the legs in place.

7. Flags: Cut two 3 x 4 1/2-inch metal rectangles for flags. Cut two 8-inch lengths of heavy wire for staffs. Drill holes for the staffs through each arm dowel 3/8 inch from the hand end. Fold and glue a short side of the flag over the staff, about 1/2 inch below the top; crimp with pliers. Bend down the 1/2 inch at the top of the staff. Let the glue dry. Then trace the flag pattern, at right. Using the transfer paper,

trace the pattern on one side of the metal, placing the blue field next to the staff. Tape the metal over scrap wood and punch a row of holes along each line of the flag with a hammer and thin nail.

8. Assembly: Cut a 5 3/4-inch length of 1/4-inch dowel for the axle. Insert the dowel through the armhole on the body; glue an arm to each end making sure the dowel can turn freely. Insert the flagstaffs into the arms, poking about 1 inch of wire through to the other side. With pliers, bend the staff in a zigzag line to secure it in place. Turn the flags to point inward or outward.

9. Painting: Paint a blue shirt and hat and white pants; let the paint dry. Mix red, white, yellow and a little blue to paint the face. Mix yellow, blue and a little black to paint the green base. Paint both sides of the flags. When dry, paint white stars on the shirt and red stripes on the pants. Paint the eyes and mouth. Let the paint dry.

10. Finishing: To give the whirligig a weathered, folk-art finish, rub the corners with sandpaper to let some wood show through. **Attach stars:** Placing the wooden stars so the spinning flags will not hit them, drill a 1/2-inch-deep hole in the base for each star wire. Glue the wires into the holes. Brush the finish on the surfaces and let it dry.

FLAG FOR WHIRLIGIG

Star-Spangled Director's Chairs

★

The basic red, white, and blue of these chairs will sparkle on the lawn or deck all summer.

- ◆ two director's chairs
- ◆ red and blue covers for the chairs
- ◆ adhesive shelving plastic
- ◆ file card or stiff paper
- ◆ white fabric paint
- ◆ paintbrush; stencil brush
- ◆ tracing paper
- ◆ masking tape
- ◆ crafts knife
- ◆ ruler
- ◆ white primer, white enamel paint, brushes and sandpaper to paint the chairs (optional)

HOW TO MAKE THEM

1. To paint the wood: Remove the canvas seat or back from the chair, but leave one piece on to keep the frame upright. Cover the hardware with tape, and sand, prime and paint the wood white following the manufacturer's instructions for the primer and paint.

2. Mark the canvas for stripes: With the ruler and pencil, mark the front of the red chair-back evenly for four stripes. **(Tip:** To divide easily, slant the ruler on the piece until you have evenly spaced numbers, such as 2, 4, 6; mark.) Mark stripes of equal width across the red seat. **Cut stencils for stars:** Trace a star from one of the patterns for the Stars-and-Stripes Bowls on page 178. Cut shelving plastic to fit the blue seat and back. Trace stars evenly spaced onto the back of the shelving plastic. On a firm cutting surface, cut out the stars with the crafts knife.

3. Paint the stripes: Cover the stripes to remain red firmly with masking tape. Paint the white stripes as many coats as needed to cover the fabric, letting each coat of paint dry. Remove the tape.

4. Paint the stars: Peel off the paper backing and stick the plastic stencil firmly to the blue chair seat and to the front of the chair back. Paint the stars with the stencil brush or flat brush, working from the edges to keep paint from seeping under the plastic. Carefully remove the plastic. Touch up the paint if necessary.

5. Mix and match: Place a blue starry seat and striped back on one chair and a striped seat and starry back on the other chair.

This pair of star-struck director's chairs might just be the biggest hit at your barbecue!

Four-Hearts Wall Hanging

★

This small hanging will look best over small furniture—a hall table, a night table or a straight chair. The patchwork could also be used as the front of a large pillow.

SIZE

19 inches square

WHAT YOU'LL NEED

- cotton or cotton-blend fabrics: ⅜ yard blue with stars; ¼ yard each red-and-white stripe and white-on-white calico; ⅛ yard of red pin dot; 18-inch square of any calico or muslin for back
- 19-inch square of thin quilt batt
- 2 yards each of red, white, and blue 6-strand embroidery floss

Four hearts, four squares, and countless stars and stripes—love of country never looked so good.

- white quilting thread
- dark blue and white sewing threads
- 3 plastic rings
- paper-backed fusible web
- embroidery needle
- quilting needle (optional)
- ruler and fabric shears
- rotary cutter and mat (optional)
- tracing paper

HOW TO MAKE IT

Sewing note: Stitch fabrics with right sides together; a ¼-inch seam allowance is included in the cutting. Press seams toward the darker fabric.

1. Pattern: Trace the half heart pattern, below, right, on folded paper, placing the fold on the center line and including the crosswise seamline. Cut on the outline through both layers.

2. Cutting: Cut four 5½-inch squares of the **white calico,** twelve 1½ x 5-inch strips of the **red stripe** (with stripes parallel to the short edge) and nine 1½-inch squares of the **pin dot.** From the **blue with stars,** cut 2 border strips 3 x 14 inches for the sides, two strips 3 x 19 inches for the top and bottom, and 4 strips 1½ x 19 inches for the binding. **Hearts:** Cut a 3 x 20-inch strip across the blue fabric and four 3 x 5-inch strips of red stripe with stripes parallel to the short edges. Stitch the red strips to the lower edge of the blue. Press the seam open. Fuse the web to the back, leaving the paper attached. Mark the seamline on the paper. Then trace and cut 4 hearts with their tops over the blue fabric, the dotted line on the seam and the red lines centered.

3. Appliqué: Center a heart on the front of each white square and mark the position lightly with pencil. Peel off the paper backing; pin and fuse the hearts to the squares, following the web manufacturer's directions for heat and timing.

4. Patchwork: Lay out the heart blocks, sashes and pin-dot squares according to the photograph. Stitch the pieces together in strips, then stitch the strips together, with the seamlines of the patchwork matching. **Borders:** Stitch the short blue borders to the side edges and trim the ends even with the patchwork. Stitch the long borders to the top and bottom.

5. Quilting: Spread out the back fabric with the wrong side facing you. Center the batt and the patchwork, right side out, on top. Starting in the center, pin or baste the pieces thoroughly together (from center to corners, then from center to sides), keeping the fabrics smooth. With white quilting thread, hand-sew short running stitches through all the thicknesses around each heart and along the seams of the sashes and pin-dot squares. Stitch a running-stitch X over each pin-dot square.

6. Embroidery: With two strands of floss, embroider cross-stitches (as for the Folk Art Holiday Wall Hanging, diagram on page 3) through one layer over the edges and crosswise seam of the hearts, using blue floss along the top of the heart, red on the bottom, and white over the crosswise seam.

7. Binding: With the right sides together, stitch a binding strip to the two side edges. Trim the ends. Fold each binding to the back; turn under and slip-stitch the edge in place. Centering the strips, bind the top and bottom edges, tucking in the ends when you fold them back. For hanging, sew rings to the top corners and the center, about 1 inch from the top edges.

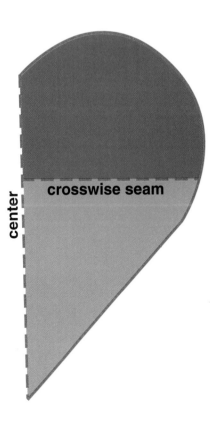

center

crosswise seam

Stars-and-Stripes Bowls

★

These lightweight bowls are as decorative as they are functional. Design your own for any holiday or just for fun. They can be decoupaged with cut and pasted papers or painted. They're a good project for a class or crafts group.

WHAT YOU'LL NEED (FOR 5)

- ◆ metal, plastic, or crockery bowls for molds
- ◆ 32 ounces Mod Podge matte sealer/glue
- ◆ newspaper or construction paper
- ◆ red, white, and blue acrylic paints
- ◆ synthetic, flat 1½-inch and smaller paint-brushes
- ◆ water-based or polyurethane clear satin finish
- ◆ plastic food wrap for lining the mold
- ◆ masking tape
- ◆ a disposable foil baking pan
- ◆ foil or plastic for the work surface
- ◆ tracing paper

HOW TO MAKE THEM

1. Prepare the mold: Cover the outside of the bowl smoothly with plastic wrap and tape the edge inside. Turn the bowl upside down on a protected work surface.

2. Mix the glue: In the disposable pan, mix Mod Podge with water, a little at a time, until the mixture is the consistency of heavy cream. Fill the pan about one-quarter full.

3. Lay the paper strips in the glue: Cut 2 x 7-inch paper strips or a size that lies well on the mold.

Lay the strips in the glue, placing one at a time so each will be completely covered in glue. Let the strips sit for about five minutes or until soaked through.

4. Apply the strips to the mold: Run a strip between two fingers to remove excess glue, and smooth the strip onto the exterior of the bowl from the rim to the center. Cover the bowl with a layer of parallel strips. Lay the next layer across them. Alternate layers in this manner, placing about 12 layers on large bowls, 8 layers on small bowls. Let the glue dry until the paper feels firm and crisp (this may take 24 to 36 hours).

5. Remove the mold: Lift off the masking tape and carefully slip the hardened papier-mâché and the plastic wrap off the bowl. Peel off the wrap. Trim the rim of the papier-mâché bowl with scissors, a crafts knife or sandpaper—and don't be too exacting; the bowl can retain an irregular, handmade look. If you want to cover the rim, add 2 layers of strips inside the bowl, bringing the ends over the rim to the outside. Then add 2 layers to the outside, without covering the rim. Let the bowl dry thoroughly.

6. Paint: Brush two coats of white paint on the interior and exterior of the bowl for the undercoat, letting each coat dry thoroughly. **Stars:** Add two

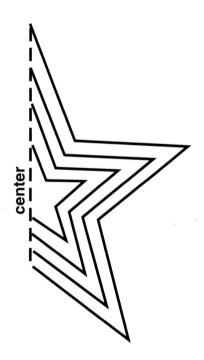

coats of red or blue as a background for white stars, or leave the bowl white for colored stars. Fold tracing paper in half, place the fold on the broken line of the star patterns on page 178, and trace each size separately. Cut out patterns through both layers and open them flat. Trace stars randomly onto the bowls with a pencil. Paint each one with a small brush. **Stripes:** Center a long, 1¼-inch-wide (or another size) clean paper strip inside a white bowl, extending from rim to rim. Trace the edges onto the bowl and remove the strip. Slide a tape measure along one edge of the stripe and make a row of dots 1¼ inches away to mark the next stripe. Connect the dots. Repeat up to the rim on each side. Leave the center stripe white and paint alternate stripes red or blue. When the paint has dried, extend the stripes to the outside.

7. Finishing: When all paint is completely dry, brush on two or three coats of finish, following the manufacturer's directions. Allow the finish to dry completely before using the bowl. To clean it, wash the bowl gently with a damp sponge and mild detergent; rinse with the sponge and dry with a towel.

Our-True-Colors T-shirts

★

Once you have the shirts and fabric paints, be as creative as you like with the placement of stars and stripes. Let the children paint some shirts too.

WHAT YOU'LL NEED

◆ a cotton or cotton-blend T-shirt
◆ red and blue fabric paints
◆ a No. 6 synthetic round watercolor brush
◆ stiff paper or light cardboard for templates
◆ heavy aluminum foil or shirt-size cardboard

◆ unprinted newsprint paper
◆ tracing paper
◆ a No. 2 pencil or disappearing fabric marker
◆ scissors
◆ ruler
◆ masking tape or clear tape

HOW TO MAKE IT

Note: Prewash and iron the T-shirts if required by the paint manufacturer.

1. Make stars-and-stripes patterns: Fold the tracing paper in half. Place the fold on the broken line of the star patterns on page 181, and trace each size star separately. Cut through both layers and open each pattern flat. Cut the patterns from stiff paper or cardboard. With a pencil and ruler draw 1-to-1¼-inch-wide patterns for stripes on the cardboard and cut out.

2. Plan the design: Fold the T-shirt in half lengthwise to find the center; mark with tape. Place

Stars and stripes T-shirts are so easy to paint, you could produce a batch for the whole family, even the whole block!

★

foil or cardboard inside the shirt to stiffen the fabric and protect the back. Smooth the front of the shirt flat. Starting at the center, measure for an even placement of stars and stripes or arrange them at random as you like. Trace the patterns on the shirt lightly with the fabric marker or pencil. (Pencil lines can be erased or rinsed out later.)

3. Paint: Using a slightly damp brush, start at the top and paint the shapes, following the grain of the fabric on stripes and other straight lines. **To prevent mistakes:** It's easy to get paint where you don't want it. Tape paper over unpainted areas to protect them. Wash off any unwanted spots with soap and water before the paint dries, or incorporate them into the design. Let the finished design dry flat, then remove the foil or cardboard.

4. Press: Heat-set the paint if required by the paint manufacturer.

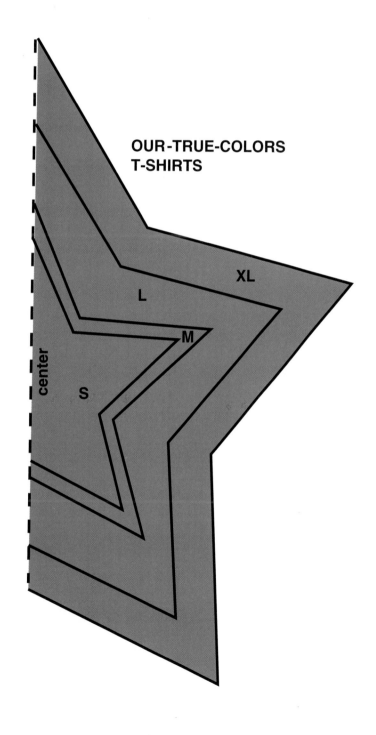

OUR-TRUE-COLORS T-SHIRTS

Paint ready-made birdhouses and add lights for a festive twinkle at a window or on a table.

Sparkling Birdhouses

★

After the party's over, hang the birdhouses outside but omit the lights, since the birds may peck the wires.

- ◆ wooden birdhouse with a removable bottom
- ◆ red, white, and blue acrylic paints
- ◆ short string of red, white, and blue lights with battery power and switch
- ◆ drill with ⅜-inch-diameter bit
- ◆ flat foam or bristle paintbrushes
- ◆ masking tape
- ◆ fine sandpaper
- ◆ duct tape or electrical tape
- ◆ fabric star appliqués and white glue (optional)

1. Drill holes for the lights: Following the photograph for suggested placement, drill ⅜-inch-diameter holes in the house front for the light bulbs. Remove all but one screw from the underside, or otherwise attach the bottom so you can easily swivel or remove it to install the lights and reach the switch.

2. Paint the house white: Sand the wood lightly along the grain. Dust off the residue. Brush on two or three coats of white paint, letting each coat dry thoroughly.

3. Add designs: Outline straight or zigzag stripes and other decorations on the house with pencil. Mask the edges of straight lines with tape. Paint the designs red or blue. Remove the tape and let the paint dry. Glue appliqués to the outside.

4. Install the lights: Insert lights through the holes from the inside and tape them in position. Place the battery and switch inside, and open the bottom to reach the switch to turn the lights on and off. Or make an exit hole for the wire and place the switch on the outside.

Tip: Whimsical birdhouses seem to enchant year after year. Paint a few in bright colors, others in drab colors, hang them outside and see which ones the birds prefer.

All-American Quilt

★

This beautiful quilt could be the first one you make. It requires fabric in only three colors, and is cleverly assembled from long strips of fabric—not little squares. All the cutting, stitching and machine-quilting is done in straight lines.

Approximately 72 x 87 inches

◆ plain or print 45-inch-wide cotton or cotton-blend fabrics (see Fabric Note, above, right) of 2 yards each of blue and red and 3 yards of white for the quilt top and 5 yards red (or another color) for the back

◆ 90 x 108-inch quilt batt

◆ 2 large spools white cotton or cotton-wrapped thread

◆ quilt pins or large safety pins

◆ transparent ruler at least 3 inches wide

◆ fabric shears

◆ rotary cutter and pad (optional)

Fabric Note: Closely woven fabrics can be torn into strips, making the work faster. Looser weaves will fray beyond the ¼-inch seam allowance and should be cut. Test by tearing a strip across the fabric.

Stitching note: For best results, it is important to cut and stitch accurately. To stitch seams, pin the pieces with the right sides together and guide them along the mark for ¼-inch seam allowance on your machine. (If your machine is not marked, use masking tape to make a guideline to the right of the machine needle.) Press the seam allowances to one side after each step.

1. Prewash the fabrics: Wash and iron the cotton fabrics, to shrink them and remove any excess dye. Wash dark colors separately, since they may run.

2. Cut the fabric strips: Cut off 1 yard of blue fabric and set it aside for borders. Clip into the selvage of the quilt-top fabrics horizontally every 3 inches and tear or cut across to make eighteen 3 x 45-inch strips each from the red, white, and blue fabrics. Then cut or tear 5 more red, 5 blue, and 18 white 3-inch-wide strips across the fabric. Cut these strips in half crosswise to have 10 red, 10 blue, and 36 white 3 x 22½-inch strips. (Discard the tenth red and blue strips.) Keep the colors and sizes separate.

3. Stitch the strips into units: Following the color sequences in unit diagrams 1, 2, 3, and 4, page 186, stitch together twenty-seven 45-inch strips each on long edges to make units A and C (repeat the bracketed sequence on the diagrams three more times). Stitch together the twenty-seven 22½-inch

This quilt—easier than it looks—connects traditional nine-patch blocks in a handsome allover design.

strips each for units B and D. Each unit is 68 inches wide. Label the units.

4. Cut the units into strips: Now cut 3-inch-wide strips across the units at a right angle to the seams (see Step 5 on Diagram 1), omitting selvages: cut 12 from unit A, 10 from unit C, 6 from unit B, 5 from unit D. Each strip of squares is 68 inches long. Keep the strips separate in units.

5. Assemble the top: Carefully aligning the seams of the squares (tiny discrepancies are okay), pin and stitch the strips together one at a time in the following order: 1 strip A, 1 B, 1 A, 1 C, 1 D, 1 C (see Diagram 6 below, and the assembly photograph on page 187). Repeat this sequence four times more, then add 1 strip A, 1 B, and 1 A (33 rows) to form a patchwork approximately 68 x 82½ inches.

6. Border: Cut or tear eight 3½ x 45-inch strips across the blue border fabric. Stitch the strips together in pairs to make four long strips. Press the seams open. Centering the seams, stitch a strip to each side edge (longer edge) of the patchwork; trim

the ends even with the patchwork. Stitch the remaining strips to the top and bottom edges, including the ends of the borders. Trim the ends even with the outer edges of the side borders.

7. Back: Fold the 5 yards of backing fabric in half with the raw edges together. Cut along the fold. Stitch the pieces side by side on the long edges. Press the seam allowance open.

8. Assembly: Spread the back out wrong side up (on the floor if necessary). Center the batt, then the patchwork, right side out, on top. Working from the center out, pin the layers together smoothly and securely with quilt pins or safety pins (or baste with needle and thread), pinning or stitching from center out to corners and center of sides, then as needed. Avoid placing safety pins in every third seam, which will be quilted. Starting from a short edge, roll up the quilt wrong side out and place it under the sewing-machine arm ready for quilting.

9. Machine quilting: Slightly release the pressure on the presser foot of the sewing machine.

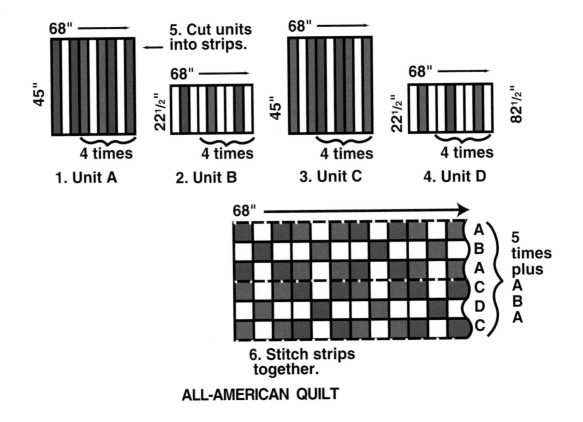

6. Stitch strips together.

ALL-AMERICAN QUILT

Set the stitch length for about 10 per inch. *(To begin and end stitching,* backstitch carefully or take 4 or 5 stitches in place at zero stitch setting; clip thread ends close to the stitching.) Unrolling the quilt row by row to sew, topstitch through all thicknesses along the seam between the border and patchwork. Then stitch along the seam between every **three** rows of squares (see the broken lines across Diagram 6). Stop occasionally to make sure the back is smooth. End with the second border seam. We did not quilt

the lengthwise seams, but you can if you like, stitching every third seam as before. Be sure to keep the fabric smooth.

10. Finishing: Topstitch through all thicknesses ¾ inch in from the outer edge of the border (2½ inches from the patchwork). Trim the back and batting to the stitched line. Fold under ¼ inch on the border edge, then fold excess border to the back of the quilt. Hand-sew or topstitch the border in place.

Patriotic Mailbox

Mailboxes can differ, so adjust the width of the blue field or the placement of the stars to the size of your mailbox. The painting technique can be adapted to any design.

WHAT YOU'LL NEED

◆ mailbox, 6½ x 19 inches or any size
◆ red, white, and blue exterior paint for metal and paintbrushes, or spray paint
◆ adhesive shelving plastic
◆ sandpaper
◆ painter's masking tape
◆ tracing paper
◆ primer (for metal if box is unpainted)
◆ tape measure
◆ scissors

HOW TO MAKE IT

1. Apply the undercoat: Mask the hardware on the box with tape. Sand the box lightly to accept paint and dust off the residue. Following the manufacturer's instructions for the primer and paint, brush primer on the entire mailbox, letting it dry with the door open. Paint the mailbox white, again letting it dry with the door open.

2. Cut stars: Trace the largest star pattern for the Stars-and-Stripes Bowls on page 178 on folded tracing paper and cut it out through both layers; open the pattern flat. Trace six stars onto the back of the shelving plastic and cut them out.

3. Paint the blue field: Following the photograph, outline a 4-inch-wide blue field on the side and top at the front end of the box with pencil and tape measure. Place painter's tape firmly along the outer edge of the line. Protect the rest of the box sides with taped-down paper if using spray paint.

They're all the rage—decorated mailboxes. Here's one that will look festive on the Fourth of July and all year long.

Peel off the paper backing and stick the stars evenly spaced firmly on the blue field. Paint the door and field blue. Let the paint dry to the touch and remove the star masks. Then let the paint dry thoroughly.

4. Paint the stripes: Cut a piece of shelving plastic to fit over the remaining sides and top of the box. Working from the center out, draw evenly spaced wavy stripes on the back of the plastic. Cut out the stripes and stick them to the box; remove the ones to be painted red. Cover up the blue field with tape and paper. Paint the stripes and the back of the box red. Let the paint dry, removing the masks as before.

Flag on a Bike

★

Paint looks good on baskets; the weave often helps to establish a geometric pattern. Try your own designs as well as this one.

WHAT YOU'LL NEED

◆ a straw bicycle basket (or any closely woven basket)

◆ white primer

◆ dark yellow latex or acrylic paint for the background

◆ red, white, and blue acrylic paints

◆ paintbrushes

◆ ruler and pencil

◆ masking tape

◆ clear acrylic sealer (optional)

◆ sandpaper

HOW TO MAKE IT

1. Prime the basket: Brush primer on the basket and let it dry.

2. Outline the flag: With the ruler and pencil, outline a flag on the outside as shown in the photograph following the lines of the basket weave if possible. Trace a small star from the Stars-and-Stripers Bowls, page 178, and trace it several times onto the blue field.

3. Paint the background: Cover the inner edges of the flag shape with tape and paint the rest of the outside of the basket with the yellow paint. Let the paint dry thoroughly.

4. Paint the flag. Remove the tape and paint the flag, masking the outer edges and stripes as needed.

5. Finishing: Rub the surface lightly with sandpaper for the weathered look of old folk art and spray the outside with an acrylic sealer. Or let the surface weather with time.

Ride up and down country lanes, stop to pick field flowers and carry them home in your jaunty painted bike basket.

HALLOWEEN

It's all in fun!

Witch in a Basket

⬥

This large basket can be used all year to hold fall flowers, winter boots, summer sandals or spring umbrellas. If you don't want to look at a witch all year, change the hat to turn her into a plain old maid.

WHAT YOU'LL NEED

- a bushel or other large basket
- orange, green, and purple acrylic paint for basket
- paintbrush and palette or coated paper plates
- ½ yard of 72-inch-wide black felt for arms, hat, and shoes
- 18 x 28-inch rectangle of purple cotton or other fabric for cape
- 1 pair of flesh-colored stockings or pantyhose
- striped socks or other fabric for legs
- ½ yard purple ribbon for hatband
- ¾ yard wide green ribbon for neck bow
- 12-inch wired chenille stem
- 2 ounces orange yarn for hair
- ⅝-inch black and white or plain black buttons for eyes
- scrap of white felt for teeth
- blush for cheeks
- flesh-colored thread
- polyester fiberfill stuffing
- low-temperature glue gun
- 8 x 12-inch and 2 x 5-inch stiff cardboards
- graph paper (optional)

HOW TO MAKE IT

1. Paint the basket: Using the acrylic paints, follow the photograph to paint simple patterns around the outside of the basket.

2. Make the witch's arms (one piece): Cut a 9 x 33-inch felt rectangle. Overlap the long edges ½ inch and glue them closed to form a tube, stuffing the tube with fiberfill as you go.

3. Hands: Cut off the stocking feet 5 inches from the toe end and stuff them with fiberfill. With flesh-colored thread, outline the fingers by sewing four fairly long (1¼ inch) stitches about ½ inch apart around the toe end through the hand.

4. Attach the hands to the arm: Glue one hand into one end of the arm. Check the arm's length on the basket rim before you glue on the second hand. The arm plus the hands should fit about two thirds of the way around the basket. Trim the end of the arm, if necessary, before you glue on the second hand.

5. Head: Cut two 11-inch-long tubes from the stocking legs. Insert one tube inside the other to form a double thickness and knot the lower end closed as you would tie a balloon. Stuff the head until it's about 9 inches long and 8 inches wide. Knot the top closed. **Nose:** Fold the 12-inch chenille stem framework for a 5-inch-long nose. Pad the nose with pieces of stuffing, cover it with a scrap of stocking, and sew the edges closed. Bend the tip. **Face:** Sew the nose to the face. Sew the button eyes, about ¼ inch apart, above the nose. With the thread, stitch a long curved mouth with backstitches (see Common Embroidery Stitches, page 223) digging into the stuffing. Cut two teeth from white felt and glue them to the mouth as shown in the photograph. Add blush to the cheeks.

6. Attach the arms and head to the basket: Glue the arms to the basket rim and the head to the center of the arms.

7. Hair: Wrap the yarn in layers evenly along the 12-inch width of the 8 x 12-inch cardboard. Hand-sew the strands together on one edge and cut through the strands on the opposite edge. Sew or glue the hair around the back of the head, leaving a bald spot on top. Using the same technique, make the witch's bangs on the 2 x 5-inch cardboard. Glue the bangs across the forehead.

here does a red-headed, snaggle-toothed witch go to rest when she's not soaring around on her broomstick? She plops herself down on your porch in a basket of bright shiny apples!

8. Hat: Crown: Cut a 16-inch square of felt. Fold it in half and cut diagonally from the lower outer corners to the upper fold to make a triangle. Cut off 1 inch across the point. Overlap and pin the side edges closed to form a cone about 7 inches wide at the bottom (folded flat). Trim the lower edge even; glue the sides closed. **Brim:** Cut a 14-inch square of black felt. Fold it in quarters to form a 7-inch square. Using scissors, round off the outer corners (the edge with no folds). Cut a 2½-inch-wide curve at the inner (opposite) corner. Open the brim flat. **Hat assembly:** Stuff the bottom of the cone and slip the brim over it, widening the opening if necessary, so that the brim fits about 1 inch above the base of the cone. Cut parallel slits 1 inch apart into the bottom of the cone and glue the flaps to the underside of the brim. Glue purple ribbon around the crown to form the hat band.

9. Cape: Turn under 1-inch hems on the sides and bottom of the cape fabric and glue or sew them in place. Then pleat and glue the upper edge to the arms around the witch's neck. Tie a bow of green ribbon and glue it to the front neck corners.

10. Legs: Cut the legs from socks or cut two 6 x 8-inch pieces of fabric and glue or stitch the long edges closed to form tubes. **Shoes:** Enlarge the pattern, below (see How to Enlarge Patterns, page 220). Cut out black felt shoes. Glue or stitch them together in pairs, leaving the tops open. Glue the legs into the tops of the shoes. Stuff the shoes and legs. Glue the leg tops closed and to the front of the basket as shown in the photograph. Fill the basket with apples or Halloween treats.

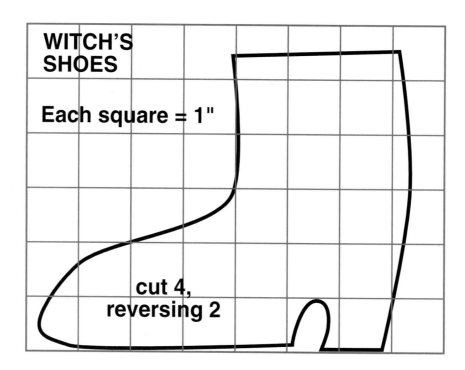

WITCH'S SHOES

Each square = 1"

cut 4, reversing 2

Jack-o'-Lanterns

"Jack-o'-lantern" was once the term for a fellow who carried a lantern—specifically, a night watchman. He evolved into a lighted pumpkin head, as scary as possible, to protect the house from evil spirits on Halloween.

HOW TO MAKE THEM

1. Cut: If you've been cutting off the top of the pumpkin to make jack-o'-lanterns, now is the time to try cutting a hole in the bottom instead. This way you can cut the base so it sits firmly and the lantern will be easier to light.

2. Scoop: Scoop out the pulp with a metal spoon and discard. Use a knife or kitchen scissors to cut through any stubborn fibers.

3. Design: Turn your pumpkin to see which side is best suited for your design. Outline a face or any other design on the pumpkin front with a felt-tip marker, a pencil or the tip of a knife. Remember to keep interior shapes such as eye pupils attached by a small "bridge" to the main shape. Carefully cut out the designs with a sharp, pointed knife. **To add pieces:** Cut ears (or other shapes you want to add) from another pumpkin or scraps. Cut a curve in the lower edges of the ears to fit against the pumpkin. Break off a piece of toothpick and insert it through the back of the ear and into the pumpkin flesh to attach the ear. (Don't leave toothpick tips showing on the inside or they may burn.) For whiskers, insert skewers (you could paint them), straw, or wires, again avoiding the flame.

4. Light: Place a votive candle in a holder, or use a thick, freestanding candle. (Make sure the candle is not too tall or it will burn the inside of the pumpkin.) Set the candle on a plate. Light the candle and place the jack-o'-lantern on top. Enjoy, but don't leave lighted candles unattended. **(Tip:** You may find small battery-operated sockets and bulbs to use instead of candles.)

Treat your jolly jack-o'-lanterns to multiple personalities—catlike, Picasso-esque—whatever suits your fancy.

*G*et into the fright-full spirit of Halloween by stringing up this bright-eyed ghost. He's guaranteed to dazzle visitors and passersby alike.

Ghost in Lights

A spectacular specter, this ghost will look equally eerie on a large tree or the front porch. You just bend wire to a simple shape and add lights.

WHAT YOU'LL NEED

◆ 5 yards of 12-gauge galvanized wire for frame

◆ 3 yards of 14- or 16-gauge galvanized wire for support

Note: Heavy wire is available on rolls in hardware stores.

- tie wire
- fish line or medium-weight wire for hanging
- strings of about 132 small, outdoor Christmas lights, preferably ones that will work if bulbs are removed
- copper sheet metal or roof flashing for eyes
- pliers
- wire snips
- metal shears or old scissors
- electrician's tape
- hammer or screwdriver
- large nail to make holes
- scrap wood or magazines
- newspapers

HOW TO MAKE IT

1. Shape the ghost: Draw a pattern for a simple ghost shape about 5 feet tall and 3 feet wide at the arms on newspapers taped together. Starting at the bottom of the ghost, bend the wire to follow the outline, using the pliers as needed to turn curves and corners. If the wire tends to flop and curl, weight the end with heavy objects or ask someone to hold it. **To end off:** Bend both ends back and hook them together. **To stabilize:** Attach the thinner wire across the frame as needed to keep it from warping. Attach wire supports for the eyes 3 inches apart across the head.

2. Make the eyes: With the metal shears or old scissors, cut two 2½ x 4½-inch ovals from copper flashing. (To make a template for an oval, draw a 1¼ x 2¼-inch rectangle for a quarter of the pattern and curve one edge.) Working on scrap wood or a pile of magazines, tape the metal in place and use the hammer and nail to punch a hole through the center of each eye large enough for one of the light bulbs. Punch pairs of smaller holes at top and bottom of each eye, centered 3 inches apart, for tie wire. Remove the tape and tap the metal surface with the hammer or handle of the screwdriver to slightly cup the eyes inward. Attach the eyes to the support wires on the ghost with tie wire through the small holes.

3. Add the lights: Placing the plug at the bottom, wind the lights around the framework up to the lower eye-support wire. (See Outdoor Lighting, page 223, for how to wind lights.) Then tape the lights along the lower eye wire, inserting a bulb, from the back, through the hole in each eye. To turn off the other bulbs around the eyes, refer to the package to make sure the string will continue to light if a bulb is removed or loosened. If not, cover unwanted lights with electrician's tape. Run the lights back along the same crosspiece and continue wrapping the frame.

4. Hang it up: Use the fish line or medium-weight wire to hang the ghost from the porch or a tree, securing the bottom as well.

Cat and Bat Banner

Seasonal banners are becoming so prevalent you'll probably feel left out if you don't hang one up. With only four pieces to appliqué, this is a beauty that's not hard to make.

SIZE

29 x 41 inches

WHAT YOU'LL NEED

◆ parachute nylon or special banner fabric: 1½ yards purple, 1 yard black, ¾ yard yellow, and ¼ yard orange
◆ thread in matching colors
◆ green and black fabric paints
◆ silk pins
◆ small round paintbrush
◆ large sheets of graph paper for patterns
◆ tracing paper
◆ straightedge, yardstick, and shears or rotary cutter, mat, and see-through ruler
◆ flagpole or a dowel and 32-inch x ¾-inch-diameter screw-in hooks for hanging
◆ sewing machine with zigzagger

*B*lack cats and bats are classic frights, so stitch up this parachute-cloth banner to hang up each year.

1. **Make the pattern:** Enlarge the pattern, below, to scale (see How to Enlarge Patterns, page 220).

2. **Cut the background:** Carefully mark and cut a 30 x 44-inch rectangle of purple fabric (see Working with Slippery Fabrics, page 222). Turn under ¼ inch on the 44-inch side edges twice; pin and topstitch. Repeat on the 30-inch lower edge. For the top rod pocket, fold under ¼ inch, then 1½ inches. Stitch across the banner ⅛ inch from the first fold.

3. **Cut out the designs:** Trace each shape from the pattern. Pin the pattern to the appropriate-color fabric and cut through pattern and fabric on the outline. With matching thread, stitch about ⅛ inch in from the edges of the curved shapes, such as the fence and moon, to prevent stretching.

4. **Appliqué:** Pin the **orange fence** across bottom of the purple background, turning ½ inch on the straight edges to the back of the purple. Topstitch along the previous seamlines with orange thread, then trim the seam allowance. Set the zigzagger for ⅛-inch-wide x ⅛-inch-long stitches and stitch in orange thread over the scalloped edge of the fence. (See The Art of Appliqué, page 222, for more details on stitching.) Pin the **moon** in place following the pattern and zigzag the edges with yellow thread. In the same manner, add the **cat** and **bat** appliqués and zigzag-stitch them to the banner with black thread.

5. **Paint:** Paint green eyes on the cat. When the paint has dried, paint black pupils.

6. **Hang:** Insert the flagpole or dowel through the rod pocket. If you are not putting the banner on a flagpole, position hooks near the ends of the dowel to support it.

CAT AND BAT BANNER
Each square = 2"

W hat guest wouldn't enter smiling when he or she sees (and probably steps over) this jolly appliquéd felt mat made in bright fall colors?

Jack-o'-Lantern Welcome Mat

This felt mat will look equally welcoming as a doormat or a wall hanging. Hang it up if you want to protect it from a puppy's teeth, cat's claws, or people's muddy shoes.

SIZE

25 x 36 inches

WHAT YOU'LL NEED

◆ 1 yard each of 72-inch-wide black and orange felt
◆ ⅓ yard of 72-inch-wide gold felt
◆ scrap of green felt
◆ orange, gold and green thread
◆ 3 yards of paper-backed fusible web
◆ 24 x 36-inch paper for pattern

- transfer paper
- black felt-tip marker
- fabric marker
- pinking shears
- small sharp scissors
- sewing machine with zigzagger

1. Cut out the pumpkins: Enlarge the pattern, below (see How to Enlarge Patterns, page 220). Transfer the pattern to orange felt (see How to Transfer Patterns, page 220) and cut out the pumpkin, omitting the stem. Cut a black pumpkin, including the stem, *½ inch larger* than the orange one all around.

2. Cut out the appliqués: Trace separate patterns for eyes, nose, mouth, letters and stem with the black marker. Before you cut them from felt, fuse web to the back of 12 x 40-inch blocks of black and gold felt, a 14 x 16-inch block of orange felt, and a scrap of green felt, leaving the paper backing on. Transfer the patterns to the paper backing of the gold or orange felt as on the pattern (be sure to trace the letters reversed). Now cut the felt pieces.

3. Fuse appliqués to black felt: Following the web manufacturer's directions, fuse the letters, eyes, and nose to the front of the black web-backed felt, leaving ¾ inch between pattern pieces. With the fabric marker, draw a line ¼ inch outside each piece on the black felt. Cut the pieces apart outside the lines, then cut on the lines with the pinking shears. To pink evenly, cut steadily forward to make each cut complete. Start the next cut at the end of the previous one.

4. Appliqué the mouth: Arrange and fuse the letters to the gold mouth. Remove the paper from the back of the black mouth. With orange thread and fairly small, open zigzag stitches (about ¹/₁₆ x ¹/₁₆ inch) stitch along the edge of the orange letters (see The Art of Appliqué, page 222, for more information).

5. Appliqué the pumpkin: Fuse the stem to the black pumpkin, ½ inch in from top and sides. Zigzag-stitch over the stem's edges using green thread. Fuse the black-backed eyes, nose, and mouth to the orange pumpkin. Center the orange pumpkin on the black one, leaving a ½-inch black border; pin. With gold thread, zigzag-stitch the edges of the eyes, nose, and mouth. With orange thread, zigzag-stitch the edges of the orange pumpkin to the black one.

6. Finishing touches: With the small straight scissors, snip a zigzag pattern in the edge of the black felt surrounding the pumpkin, making triangles that are about ⅜ inch wide. Transfer the pattern lines that define the pumpkin sections to the front, skipping over the other shapes. Stitch the lines with orange thread and long straight stitches. Press the mat under a cloth with a steam iron. Place adhesive rug tape on the back if you're putting the mat on a slippery floor.

Each square = 2"

Little Witches

These are definitely good witches—everybody loves them. Make a bunch with your friends who stitch. Give them as souvenirs at a Halloween party.

SIZE

8 inches tall seated, wearing a hat

WHAT YOU'LL NEED (FOR EACH ONE)

- 4½ x 12-inch scrap or ⅛ yard each plain bright fabric for the head and dark, patterned fabric for the body
- 4 x 4½-inch piece of contrasting fabric for legs
- two 4-inch-long wired chenille stems
- a 4-inch square of black felt for shoes
- white glue for shoes
- a scrap of black embroidery thread or dimensional fabric paint or a fine black felt-tip marker to make the eyes and mouth
- white fabric paint for teeth
- embroidery floss or yarn for hair
- polyester fiberfill stuffing
- a black hat from a crafts store (or make one from black felt)
- small basket or broom from the crafts store, or twigs and string
- small rock for weight
- masking tape
- bright-colored oven-hardening clay (optional for nose)
- glue gun for attaching a clay nose
- ribbon for bows (optional)
- tracing paper and transfer paper

HOW TO MAKE IT

1. Make the patterns: Trace the patterns on page 204. Patterns include a ¼-inch seam allowance.

2. Cut the fabrics: Transfer the patterns to the fabrics and cut them out (see How to Transfer Patterns, page 220). Cut two arms from the same fabric as the body and two legs from contrasting fabric, each 2 x 4-inch rectangles. Cut two shoes from black felt.

3. Stitch the heads to the bodies: With the right sides together, stitch each head to each body. Stitch the dart AB on the lower corners of the bodies close to the edges to shape the bottom.

*B*ubble, bubble, toil, and trouble? These chubby little witches will have none of it because they can't fly and they certainly don't sweep. In fact, as soon as you've stitched them up and plunked them down, they do nothing but sit there looking adorable.

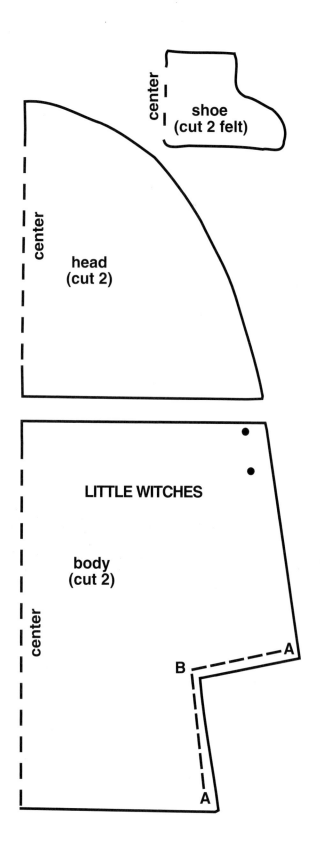

**shoe
(cut 2 felt)**

**head
(cut 2)**

LITTLE WITCHES

**body
(cut 2)**

4. Stitch arms and legs: Press the arm and leg strips in half lengthwise, right side out. Fold the long edges in to meet at the center. Fold up ¼ inch at one end of the arms (hand end). Topstitch the folded edges on each piece closed. Insert a chenille stem into each arm and trim it ½ inch shorter than the arm. With right sides together and raw edges matching, baste the raw edges of the arms to the sides of the body front between the dots.

5. Assemble the witch: With right sides together, stitch the back to the front, leaving a 2-inch-wide opening in the center of the bottom. Turn the witch right side out. Cover the small rock with masking tape. Then stuff the body firmly, placing the rock near the bottom for weight. At the opening, turn in the raw edges. Place the ends of the legs ¼ inch into the opening, leaving about ½ inch between the legs. Sew the opening closed by hand. Trim the legs to 3½ inches long. Fold and glue the shoes over the ends of the legs.

6. Make the face: Form a clay nose about 1½ inches long and ⅜ inch in diameter. Bake it as directed on the package, or stitch and stuff a cone of fabric for the nose. Mark the position of the nose with the pencil about ¾ inch above the body at the center front. Paint, embroider, or draw a black V-shaped mouth and dots for eyes. Paint two white teeth. Glue the clay nose or sew the fabric nose in place.

7. Add the hair: Cut several 10-inch strands of yarn or floss. Tie them together at the center. Sew or glue them across the head in front of the seam. Trim the ends evenly or unevenly.

8. Finishing touches: Glue the hat to the head. Add bows to the neck or hat if you like. Bend the "hands" around a basket or broom handle or a bundle of twigs tied with string.

Tombstone

Put ancient dates on the tombstone to give the cemetery a properly historic quality.

WHAT YOU'LL NEED (FOR EACH ONE)

◆ ¼-inch-thick plywood about 18 x 24 inches

◆ 30 inches of 1 x 2-inch pine for a stake

◆ black and white acrylic paint

◆ primer (optional)

◆ ¼-inch and 2-inch flat paintbrushes

◆ graph paper for pattern

◆ transfer paper

◆ sponge

◆ ¾-inch nails

◆ wood glue

◆ saber saw

◆ jars or pans for mixing colors

HOW TO MAKE IT

1. Design and cut: Draw a tombstone pattern on graph paper to fit the wood using simple shapes of your own design. Curve or point the top, making it as plain or fancy as you like. Transfer the outline to wood and cut it out with the saber saw (see Making Wooden Cutouts, page 221).

2. Paint: Brush on primer and let it dry. Mix a light gray paint (1 part black to 2 parts white). Paint the tombstone. When the paint has dried, mix a darker gray and dab it on with the sponge to suggest a stony texture. Transfer the designs from your pattern to the front and paint them black or very dark gray.

3. Attach the stake: Cut a point in the bottom of the stake. Glue and nail the stake to the center back of the plaque, flush with the top. Push the stake into the ground.

*G*et a little ghoulish and turn your yard into a cemetery for a day. Make one plaque or a yardful. You only have to cut a simple wooden shape, paint with mixtures of black and white, and decorate as you like.

Fluttering Ghost Wind Sock

When this ghost flutters, people notice. You could make it from an old sheet instead of nylon and use paint or markers instead of iron-on appliqués to draw the face.

SIZE

13 x 35 inches

WHAT YOU'LL NEED

- 1 yard of white parachute nylon or other lightweight fabric
- scrap of black cotton fabric for the eyes and mouth
- 8-inch square of paper-backed fusible web
- ¾ yard of 1½-inch-wide white grosgrain ribbon
- 9 x 12-inch piece of white felt
- ¾ yard size 4 or 5 picture wire
- 1½ yards cord for hanging
- white thread
- masking tape
- glue gun (optional)

HOW TO MAKE IT

1. Body: Cut two 13 x 36-inch pieces from the white fabric (see Working with Slippery Fabrics, page 222) if using parachute nylon.

2. Face: Following the web manufacturer's directions, fuse the web to the back of the black fabric leaving the paper backing on. Draw simple eyes and a mouth freehand on the web's paper backing. Then cut them out and peel off the backing. Using a press-

Every little breeze will make our wind sock ghost do an eerie dance —the perfect welcome to your haunted house.

ing cloth over synthetic fabrics, fuse the eyes and mouth to the center front of one white piece, placing the eyes about 5 inches below the top. Fuse the mouth about 3 inches below.

3. Hands: Draw a simple hand shape about 3 inches wide x 4 inches long and cut two from white felt. Cut the white ribbon in half for the arms. Glue or stitch a hand to one end of each ribbon. Pin the arms at a slight outward slant to the sides of the body front about 14 inches below the top. Trim the ends of the ribbons even with the side edges.

4. Assembly: With the right sides together, baste the sides of the ghost's front and back together with a ⅜-inch seam allowance. Stitch the seams and remove the basting. **Casing:** Turn under 1 inch at the top and stitch ⅛ inch from the raw edge, leaving a 1½-inch opening. Insert the wire through the casing overlapping the ends to form a circle. Twist the ends together and cover them with masking tape. Sew the opening closed. **Bottom:** Cut a 10-inch-long slit in the lower edge every 2 inches. Cut a point at the end of each strip. **Cord:** Cut 3 equal lengths of cord for hanging the wind sock. Make a knot at one end of each cord. Sew the knots, evenly spaced, inside the top of the ghost. Tie the free ends together and hang the ghost from a nail on the front porch, a flagpole, or the branch of a tree.

Tip: If your fabric tends to fray at the cut edges, trim it with pinking shears or zigzag-stitch along the edges. When using markers or paint, practice first on scrap fabric and protect your working surface with plastic or aluminum foil.

The biggest creepy-crawly of them all: a fat, black spider in a spectacular web spun from surveyor's tape.

Front-Porch Spider

Probably because it's so unusual, this is one of our most popular Halloween decorations. You could use string instead of orange tape to make the web nearly invisible, like a real spider's web.

SIZE

The spider is about 13 inches tall

WHAT YOU'LL NEED

- 1 yard black parachute nylon
- 2 x 4-inch scrap of yellow felt
- 2 each flat 1¾-inch white and ¾-inch red buttons for eyes
- about 4 yards of stiff, bendable wire to cut into pieces for the legs
- a black shoelace or 20-inch cord
- 7-inch black cord or ¼-inch-wide grosgrain ribbon for the hanging loop
- black and yellow thread
- polyester fiberfill stuffing

- pinking shears
- wire snips
- a roll of surveyor's tape (from a hardware store)
- plastic tape or pushpins or staple gun and staples to hang the tape

HOW TO MAKE IT

1. Spider's body: With the pinking shears, cut a 15 x 23-inch piece of nylon. Fold it in half, wrong side out, with short edges together, and pin. Following the diagram, at lower right, draw a curve (trace a large plate) along the upper edge of the nylon for the top of the spider; cut the curve through both layers. Fold the 7-inch cord in half to create a loop for hanging the spider. Pin the cord between the layers at the center top (X), with the ends on raw edges. With a ½-inch seam allowance, stitch the curved edge and open side closed, stopping at the dot 1 inch above the lower edge.

Casing: Fold 1 inch at the lower edge of the body to the wrong side; stitch ¾ inch from the edge, leaving the ends open.

Legs: Cut eight 4 x 16-inch nylon strips. Fold each in half lengthwise, wrong side out. Following the leg diagram, at one end of each leg, cut a point from side to fold and stitch the long edge and point closed. Turn each leg right side out. Insert a 16-inch wire, bending the ends of the wire back so they don't poke through the legs. Stuff the legs lightly with fiberfill. With the seam centered in the back, turn in ½ inch at the open end of each leg and stitch the end closed.

Attach the legs: Leaving a 6-inch space across the front of the body for a face, pin a leg at each side 4 inches above the lower edge. Arrange the others around the back, evenly spaced, alternately 5 inches and 4 inches above the lower edge. Stitch the tops of the legs to the body. Then fold the legs upward and stitch them to the body from their undersides 1 inch above the joinings. Curve the legs downward.

Eyes: Sew a red button over each white one and sew eyes onto the correct position on the face.

Mouth: Cut two 1¼ x 2-inch felt triangles. Place them side by side on the spider as shown in the photograph and sew the edges in place.

Finishing: Insert the shoelace or cord through the casing. Stuff the body firmly. Gather the bottom and insert a piece of black nylon under the opening to hide the stuffing completely. Tie the cord.

2. Web: How you arrange this depends on the space you have. (If you're using an adhesive tape to hold the web, try it out to make sure it can support the surveyor's tape and spider, and doesn't pull off porch paint when removed.) Following the photograph, hang several strips together at one corner, using tape, pins or staples. Spread out the strips and attach the ends to a porch post and rail or to the floor in a fan shape. Then hang separate strips about a foot apart halfway along a beam above the web, weave them through the other strips, and fasten the ends to the side of the porch.

3. Attach the spider: Hang the spider in the next space in front of the web from a length of tape or string inserted through the hanging loop, as if he were spinning the next strand of web. Arrange the rear legs in the web.

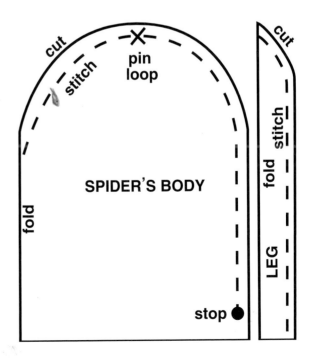

$\mathcal{M}$ix painted wood and natural branches to make a pretty, portable planter. Fill it with dried moss, potted fall flowers, Indian corn, and gourds.

Rustic Planter

A wooden bottom and ends make this a sturdy planter you can move from sun to shade and back. Fill it with seasonal plants. After autumn, you can remove the pumpkins, which are simply glued to one side.

SIZE

Bottom, 10 x 28 inches; height, 15 inches

WHAT YOU'LL NEED

FOR THE PLANTER:
- ½-inch-thick plywood, one piece 10 x 27 inches for bottom and two each 10 x 15 inches for ends
- 7 straight 28-inch-long branches, approximately 1 inch in diameter
- two 1½-inch drywall screws
- twenty-four 1½-inch nails
- wood glue
- sandpaper
- primer
- brown acrylic paint
- flat paintbrush
- drill
- saw

FOR THE PUMPKINS:
- three 9 x 10-inch pieces of ¼-inch-thick plywood
- orange and green acrylic paint
- masking tape
- glue gun
- saber saw

HOW TO MAKE IT

1. Cut off the corners of the end pieces: Following the planter diagram, mark the sides of the two 10 x 15-inch wood pieces 7 inches from the bottom. Mark the tops 4 inches in from each corner. Draw a diagonal line from each side mark to the nearest top mark. Cut along the lines with the saw.

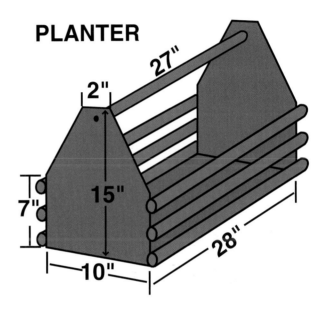

PLANTER

2. Add the bottom: On the outside of each end piece, mark the placement of four nails ¼ inch above the lower edge and evenly spaced across. Apply a little glue to the 10-inch edges of the bottom piece. Butt and nail the planter end pieces against the bottom, with outer edges flush. Let the glue dry.

3. Screw on the handle: One inch below the center top of each end piece, mark the position of a screw. Trim one branch to 27 inches long to fit between the ends. Glue the branch in place between the marks. Predrill a pilot hole for the screws at each mark through the wood and into the ends of the branch. Insert screws.

4. Nail on the side rails: Sand the edges of the planter. (Fill any holes with putty before sanding.) Then, following the diagram, glue and nail three branches to each side of the planter, predrilling nail holes.

5. Pumpkins: Enlarge the pumpkin pattern or draw a pumpkin to fit on the 9 x 10-inch pieces of plywood (see How to Enlarge patterns, page 220). Cut out the pattern and trace it onto one of the pieces of plywood. With the pattern on top, stack and tape or clamp the three pieces of plywood together. Cut all three pumpkins at once with the saber saw. Sand the edges smooth.

6. Paint: Apply primer to the plywood parts of the planter (not the branches) and to the pumpkins. Let the pieces dry. Paint the planter ends and bottom brown. Paint the pumpkins orange. When the orange is dry, paint the stems green. Glue the pumpkins to one side of the planter with the glue gun.

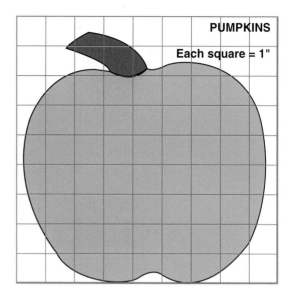

PUMPKINS

Each square = 1"

Tip: Adapt the planter to your locale or seasonal changes by cutting local flower shapes (sunflowers, cactus, daisies) to use instead of pumpkins. If you don't have available branches, you can use lattice strips for the planter sides and a dowel for the handle.

Painted Pumpkins

Why not throw a pumpkin-painting party? Acrylic paint dries fast, so all the pumpkins can be taken home when the party is over.

WHAT YOU'LL NEED

- a pumpkin
- acrylic paints
- fall leaves
- foam or bristle paintbrushes
- coated paper plates or paint pans
- paper or stencil paper for patterns
- checkerboard stencil
- clean paper or plastic to cover the work surface

HOW TO MAKE THEM

1. Make a leaf pattern: Trace leaves onto paper or onto stencil material. Simplify the shapes if the edges are intricate. You can use the patterns as masks to paint around or as stencils to paint through.

2. Transfer the leaves to pumpkins: Cut out the shapes and trace them onto the pumpkins with a pencil. Or lightly tape the mask or stencil onto each pumpkin.

3. Paint the design: Paint around the shape as shown on the green-and-blue-painted pumpkins, or fill in the shape with color, as on the checkered pumpkin and the lower right pumpkin with multi-colored leaves. If using a stencil, brush away from, not toward, the edges, so the paint doesn't seep underneath. Then carefully lift off the stencil. Place the pumpkin on a clean piece of paper or plastic-covered surface to dry.

*F*ill a basket with wheat, pinecones, branches, and small pumpkins made even more colorful with painted designs.

Bat Wind Socks

*You don't have to be batty to hang up these tree orna-
ments. They're not hard to make and will look appro-
priately scary on Halloween or at other times for true
bat lovers.*

SIZE

10½ inches long

WHAT YOU'LL NEED (FOR EACH ONE)

◆ ⅜ yard of black, closely woven, synthetic
   lining or parachute nylon
◆ black thread
◆ violet, silver and jade glitter fabric paint
◆ white and black dimensional paint in
   nozzle-tipped squeeze-bottles
◆ small paintbrush
◆ four 12-inch wired chenille stems
◆ black embroidery thread or crochet thread
   for hanging
◆ masking tape
◆ white transfer paper
◆ large sheet of cardboard or paper

Silver-toothed bat
wind socks are a sterling way to
trace the autumn wind's course,
and they are good for a few
giggles or squeals, too.

1. Cut the fabrics: Enlarge the wing and ear patterns, below (see How to Enlarge Patterns, page 221). Transfer the patterns to fabric and cut them out. Also cut two 6 x 12-inch fabric rectangles for the body.

2. Stitch the wings: Fold each wing in half wrong side out and stitch the curved edges closed, taking care not to stretch the fabric, with ¼-inch seam allowance. Clip into the seam allowance at the points and on the curves; turn right side out. Top-stitch ½ inch from the folded edge to form a casing for wire. Insert a wired stem in each casing; trim the wire ¼ inch shorter than the casing.

3. Stitch the ears: With right sides together, stitch the ears together in pairs, leaving the bottoms open. Turn right side out. Tuck in the raw edges and sew the bottom closed.

4. Paint the face: Tape the body front to cardboard or paper for painting. Transfer the face from the pattern. Paint the eyes green and the mouth white. When the paint has dried, paint black pupils and silver teeth. Paint the front of each ear violet, leaving a border of black.

5. Assembly: With right sides together, pin a wing on each side edge of the bat front ¾ inch below the top with raw edges matching. Fold wings in to fit over the body and pin the back, wrong side out, on top. Stitch the side seams. **Casings:** Fold ¾ inch at the top and bottom of the body to the wrong side. Stitch ½ inch from folds, leaving a 2-inch opening for a wired stem. Insert the stems in each casing to form a circle and tape the ends together. Stitch the openings closed. Turn the wind sock right side out. **Ears:** Stitch the bottom of the ears behind the top of the front. **To hang:** With a large-eyed needle, evenly space and pull four 15-inch (or longer) strands of embroidery thread from the inside out through the bottom casing to hang the bat upside down or through the top to hang it right side up. Knot the lower ends around the casing and tie the free ends together. Fold the wings to the sides, bat style, or leave them open if the bat is right side up.

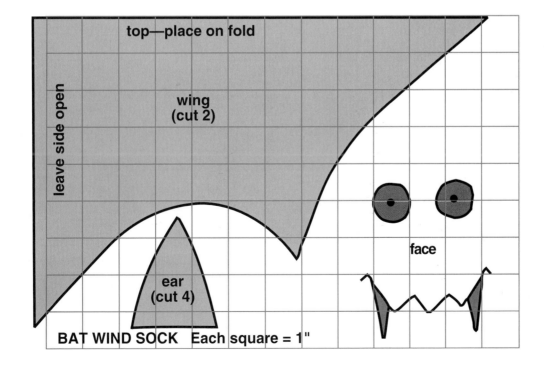

top—place on fold

leave side open

wing
(cut 2)

ear
(cut 4)

face

BAT WIND SOCK   Each square = 1"

Pumpkin-People Scarecrows

🎃

As your garden beds down, these wooden pumpkin people will liven it up until snow falls.

About 4 feet tall

·

- ♦ ½ sheet (48 x 48 inches) of ½-inch-thick plywood
- ♦ primer
- ♦ acrylic paints in red, blue, turquoise, orange, yellow, green, white, and black
- ♦ 1-inch and 2-inch sponges or bristle brushes
- ♦ size 5 round paintbrush
- ♦ sandpaper
- ♦ 1-inch galvanized flat-head wood screws
- ♦ white glue
- ♦ two 1-inch-wide butt hinges for each stand
- ♦ paper for patterns
- ♦ clear polyurethane or water-resistant finish
- ♦ yardstick or large T square
- ♦ drill
- ♦ saber saw

1. Enlarge the patterns: With the yardstick or square, draw a 4-inch grid on paper or directly on the wood, including the outlines for the face and the main lines of the clothes (see How to Enlarge Patterns, page 220). Place the pieces as close together as possible. Enlarge the arm, foot, and crow patterns on paper, cut out the patterns and trace the arms (each pair is one piece), two feet for each figure, and several crows on the wood.

2. Cut the pieces from wood: See Making Wooden Cutouts, page 221.

3. Paint and assemble the pieces: Brush primer on all the pieces, except the stands. Using the photograh as a guide, paint the main color areas. When the paint has dried, position the arms and start two screw holes with the drill. Screw the arms across the back. With 2 screws each attach a few crows to the arms. (Save a few crows to place on the ground.) Glue and screw the feet in place with 2 screws each. Paint the details freehand (patches, buttons, face, hatband, plaid).

4. Finishing: Apply varnish to the entire piece and the stand. Mark the center back for placement of the stand top, with the lower point of the stand extending about 6 inches below the lower edge. Screw the hinges to the edge of the stand top and to the back of the scarecrow, so the stand folds out. Cut 1 x 8-inch pointed stakes from scrap wood and screw them to the center back of additional crows to secure in the ground. Add stakes to the back at the bottom of the scarecrows if necessary.

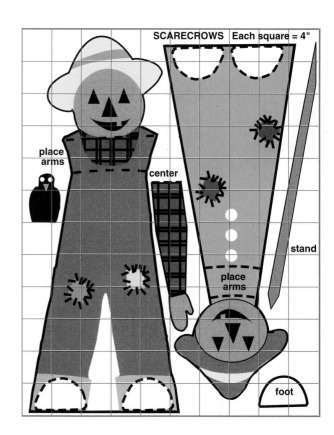

ur wooden scarecrows are a cute couple you can stand in the yard all fall, year after year. They're sure to be magnets for kids, compliments, and probably crows.

Autumn Leaves Banner

For a bit of local color and a more personalized banner, trace several kinds of local leaves to use as patterns on this banner.

SIZE

27½ x 44 inches

WHAT YOU'LL NEED

- 60-inch-wide nylon fabric (banner fabric if available): ¾ yard white, ½ yard each golden brown and orange, ¼ yard gold, and ⅛ yard each dark brown, maroon, and green
- thread: white, golden brown, and a large spool of black
- 20 x 40-inch shelf paper or pattern paper
- tracing paper
- black felt-tip marker
- masking tape or clear tape
- water-soluble fabric marker
- fine straight pins
- fabric shears
- small, sharp, pointed scissors
- yardstick
- 30-inch or longer dowel or flagpole

HOW TO MAKE IT

1. Enlarge the pattern: Refer to How to Enlarge Patterns, page 220, and copy the whole design on shelf paper or pattern paper. Darken the design lines with the black marker.

2. Cut the background and borders: Cut white fabric 24¼ x 46¾ inches. From golden brown, cut 4½-inch-wide borders, two each 46¾ inches long and one 30 inches long.

3. Trace the design onto the background: Tape the white background fabric over the pattern, centering the design. Trace the design onto the fabric with the water-soluble marker.

4. Cut out the leaves and pumpkin: Following the pattern for colors, trace the leaves and pumpkin onto the colored fabrics with the marker. Use the small scissors to cut them out.

5. Appliqué: Leaves around pumpkin: Pin the leaves that appear at the edge of the pumpkin onto the background fabric. Using black thread and a ⅛-inch-wide satin stitch in your zigzagger, slowly stitch along the outer edges of the leaves but not along the pumpkin edge. (See The Art of Appliqué, page 222, for more stitching details.) With the pointed scissors, cut away the white fabric from behind the leaves. **Pumpkin:** In the same way, appliqué the pumpkin stem, then the outer edges of the pumpkin. **Blown leaves:** Finally, appliqué the outer edges of the blown leaves. Cut white fabric from the back of the appliqués.

AUTUMN LEAVES BANNER   Top

Each square = 2"

A bright, breeze-catching banner you can make now to wave for years to come.

6. Stitch the detail lines: With black thread, satin-stitch the lines on the pumpkin and the veins on the leaves, backstitching at the beginning and end to secure the thread.

7. Iron the appliqué: Steam-press the stitched appliqué lightly under a press cloth on a low heat setting.

8. Attach the borders: Sides: With wrong sides out and raw edges together, pin the long borders to the sides of the *back* of the white fabric. With golden-brown thread, stitch ¼ inch from the edge. Press the seams open. Press ¼ inch on the long raw edges of borders toward the front. Fold borders in half to the front and pin in place, then topstitch along the front fold. **Bottom:** Center and apply the lower border to the back as before. Trim the ends to ½ inch wider than the banner and press them to the wrong side. Press the edge and stitch the border to the front as before. Topstitch the ends closed.

9. Make the rod pocket: Press ¼ inch, then 2½ inches at the top of the banner to the wrong side; pin. Stitch along the first fold, then ¼ inch above to form a double row. Press. Slip the dowel or flagpole through the pocket to hang the banner.

CRAFTS TIPS AND TECHNIQUES

Where to Buy Crafts Materials

Large crafts-supply and fabric chain stores have a dazzling array of supplies and materials. You will usually find everything you need for a project in one store—paints, fabrics, embroidery threads, dried flowers, paper, glues, clear finishes, and decorative stones, as well as materials you've never imagined. Art-supply, variety, and paint stores have added crafts supplies to their inventories. Lumberyards and home centers are sources for wood, hardware, paints, and tools. And don't forget local needlework and fabric stores, garden centers and floral suppliers. If you haven't investigated these sources before, start by looking in the yellow pages of your phone book. If you cannot find the specific supplies listed for a project, substitute similar available materials.

How to Enlarge Patterns

Patterns for projects that are larger than the pages of this book have to be enlarged on a photocopier or on graph paper.

To photocopy: Color patterns can be enlarged on black-and-white copiers as well as on color copiers. Start with the greatest enlargement on the machine, then enlarge or decrease successive copies of the pattern until the squares on the copy are the required size. (For example, if the pattern scale is "each square equals 1 inch," each square on the enlarged grid should be 1 inch square.) Very large patterns will have to be enlarged in sections. Enlarge each section to the required size, then match up the lines (trim excess paper if necessary) and tape the papers together.

To draw on a grid: This is the traditional method of making an enlargement to scale. With a pencil and ruler, on graph paper or plain paper draw a grid of squares the required size, like the grid on the pattern. In each square, copy the lines from the corresponding square of the pattern. If the pattern is complex, number each square on the pattern and your grid, to help you keep your place.

How to Transfer Patterns

After you have made full-size patterns, transfer them to your crafts materials using one of the following methods.

To use transfer paper: Transfer papers such as graphite paper, dressmaker's carbon or multipurpose paper are available in crafts, fabric, and art-supply stores. Use a transfer paper especially when there are many inner detail lines on the pattern. Place the transfer paper facedown over your material. Place the pattern face up on top and tape the edges in place with removable tape. Go over the pattern lines with a pencil or tracing wheel to transfer them. Remove the papers.

To transfer without transfer paper: 1. Pencil method: You probably learned this method in school, and it still works. Scribble lines on the back of the pattern with a soft, dark pencil. Place the pattern face up on your craft material and draw accurately over the lines. Remove the pattern. If the transferred lines are blurry, strengthen and clarify them with a pencil or marker. **2. Cut-out method:** To transfer simple shapes, cut out the traced pattern on the outline. Pin or tape the pattern in place and trace around the edge onto your craft material.

To transfer half patterns: Many of the patterns in this book are half patterns, with a broken line indicating the center of the shape. This is not just to save space; it ensures that both sides of the shape will be the same. **To transfer a half pattern to fabric:** Fold and pin the fabric in half, wrong side out. Place the center line of the half pattern on the fold and pin the pattern firmly in place. Trace the outline and cut, or simply cut along the pattern edge through both layers. **Note:** This is best used for simple shapes with no inner details. For shapes with inner detail lines, make full patterns so you can trace the details on both halves.

To make a whole pattern from a half pattern: After enlarging the pattern from the book, or when tracing a full-size half pattern from the book, fold tracing paper in half and place the fold on the center line of the pattern. Trace the outline on the top layer of the tracing paper. Cut out the tracing paper through both layers, leaving the fold uncut. Turn the folded tracing over and trace any details from the other side. Then open the pattern flat.

Making Wooden Cutouts

Make the pattern: Enlarge the pattern on paper or draw a grid to scale directly on rectangular plywood (see How to Enlarge Patterns, page 220). Include lines for details. If you're drawing the pattern directly on wood, make the lines fairly dark so they will show through the primer when it dries. Or cut out the paper pattern and transfer the outline to the wood with transfer paper.

Make a support for yard ornaments: You'll need something to brace the back of outdoor or other freestanding plaques. Cut a pointed strip for lawn ornaments, as for the Pumpkin-People Scarecrows, page 216. Or cut a large triangle with an 85-degree angle at the bottom (so the piece will tilt back slightly) for ornaments that will sit on a floor or solid ground. Cut small (2 x 8-inch) stakes to additionally support the lower edge of lawn ornaments.

Cut the wood: When sawing, wear safety goggles and a mask (available at lumberyards and paint and hardware stores) to protect your face from chips. Clamp the wood firmly on a worktable with a C-clamp (place cardboard or wood under the clamp to prevent dents), with the part you're cutting extending over the edge. Cut out the shape with the required saw. To turn corners and navigate tight curves, cut excess wood from the edge to remove small sections at a time. When drilling holes all the way through, place scrap wood behind the piece you are drilling, to keep the back of the wood from splitting and to protect the worktable.

Sand, prime, and paint the wood: Fill any large gaps in the plywood with wood putty. Let the putty dry, then sand the putty and the wood edges. Apply white primer to seal the wood (unless you are planning to apply color as a thin stain). The white background will also make the colors bright and clear when you paint. When the primer is dry, transfer detail lines from the paper pattern. Brush on the paint with foam or bristle brushes, letting each color dry to the touch before painting the adjacent color. Lay down masking tape to guide straight lines. Small details such as faces, arm outlines, and other designs can be added over dry paint.

Attach the support: Center the long, pointed stake on the back, with the point about 6 inches below the bottom, to insert in the ground, or center the triangle with its lower edge flush at the bottom. Mark the placement. Drill pilot holes for hinges and attach the support. Screw or nail additional short stakes to the back of the lower edge of lawn ornaments, if this is necessary.

Outdoor Lighting

Buy the type of outdoor lights that don't go dark when a single bulb burns out. Or make sure you have replacement bulbs handy. When arranging lights for display, plan to have the plugs near access to an outlet or outdoor extension cord. (For small projects, you may be able to use battery-operated light sets.) When outlining an ornament, buy enough lights to have approximately one bulb every 3 inches to define the shape. Wind one string around the ornament frame, letting the lights fall naturally without crowding them or making sharp turns that could break the wires. Fasten the wire to the frame with electrical tape. Wind the second string to fill in the spaces. Be sure to use only outdoor extension cords. Make exposed connections *waterproof* by covering them with electrical tape.

The Art of Appliqué

The technique of applying fabric shapes to a background is called appliqué, from the French "to put on." (If you're wondering about the pronunciation, it's *ap-lee-kay*.) Appliqué is a wonderful way to decorate quilts, clothing, stuffed toys—you name it. There are three basic ways to appliqué. Traditionally the pieces are sewn on by hand, but appliquéing can be done with a sewing machine, and for real speed, with iron-on fusible web or bonding material.

To sew by hand: Draw designs on fabric and add ¼ inch or less to turn under around the edge. Cut out the shapes with small, sharp scissors, so you can get all the details. Press or fold the edges under (clip slits in curved edges and trim corners, if they won't lie flat) and baste the pieces to the background fabric. Sew the appliqué in place along its fold with slip stitches or decorative embroidery.

To stitch by machine: Cut out the exact fabric shape for the appliqué, without adding seam allowance. Baste it (or fuse with web) in place and zigzag-stitch by machine carefully over the raw edges. Start with the needle at the outer edge, ready for an inward stitch. The width of the stitches should suit the size of the appliqué. When you turn corners, be sure to have the needle positioned correctly in the fabric for the next zig or zag. Or fasten off, pull threads to the back, and start again in the new direction. To apply materials that have finished edges, such as ribbon or felt, you can topstitch near the edges with straight stitches instead of zigzagging.

To iron on with fusible web: Paper-backed webs and adhesives allow you to bond the appliqué shapes in place with your iron. There are also special glues. This eliminates basting (tedious to many) and holds the appliqué firmly in place when you zigzag-stitch over the edge. Webs and iron-on adhesives come in various lengths and weights, with all the directions you need for application. They may add the merest stiffness to the appliqué, but this is acceptable on all but the most delicate pieces. To eliminate sewing altogether, the edges of ironed-on appliqués can be outlined with dimensional fabric paint. This covers the raw edges and holds the appliqué in place. And on projects that don't have to be laundered frequently (like curtains), you can let the raw edges be part of the look.

Working with Slippery Fabrics

Silky nylon fabrics, such as those for the banners and wind socks may slip and slide as you cut and stitch them. Thin fabrics and laces may catch in the machine. To prevent this, pin tissue paper or baste tear-away stitching fabric to the back. Leave the backing in place while marking, cutting and stitching the fabric (but remove it from the back of appliqués before stitching them in place). Then snip a hole in the backing material and tear it away gently by hand along the stitched lines.

Projects with Slippery Fabrics

Common Embroidery Stitches

Backstitch

Blanket Stitch

Fly Stitch

French Knot (triple wrap)

Lazy Daisy Stitch

Satin Stitch

Running Stitch

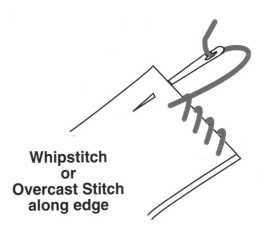

Whipstitch or Overcast Stitch along edge

Straight Stitch

CRAFTS TERMS

Acrylic paint: A durable paint in a wide range of colors; it can be thinned with water to any degree, and it dries quickly. Use it with synthetic or foam brushes. Wash brushes with soap and water before the paint dries.

Banner fabric: A nonfading, thin nylon often labeled "banner fabric" in stores.

Clear finish: Any varnish to protect paint and wood surfaces, such as clear polyurethane. When possible, use a water-based finish for easy cleanup and a water-resistant or exterior finish for outdoor projects.

Clip corners: Cut diagonally across the seam allowance on stitched corners to make them sharp when turned right side out.

Clip curves: Clip from the edge into the seam allowance at intervals on stitched curved edges to make the edge smooth when turned right side out.

Crafts glue stick: White or clear glue in stick form (not to be confused with glue sticks for glue guns); excellent for gluing paper smoothly in place.

Crafts knife: A knife with changeable fine, sharp, pointed blades, such as an X-Acto knife.

Decoupage: Decoration made from cut and pasted papers.

Dimensional paint: Crafts paint or fabric paint applied from a nozzle-tipped squeeze-bottle to achieve a raised line.

Duct tape: A strong, silver-colored fabric tape.

Fabric paint: A flat or dimensional paint made especially to bond smoothly to fabric and be washed without fading.

Fish line: A clear, nylon monofilament suitable for tying and hanging materials.

Flat paintbrush: Brush with a tip cut straight across.

Florist's picks: Wooden picks in various lengths for attaching materials to flower arrangements.

Foam paintbrush: An inexpensive sponge brush, it can be used instead of a bristle brush, especially for applying glues and smooth finishes.

Glue gun: An electrical, gun-shaped instrument with special glue that is applied hot and acts as an instant bond for bulky materials. Use a low-temperature gun and glue for most crafts projects.

Grain of fabric: The crosswise and lengthwise direction of the woven threads.

Graph paper: Paper ruled with light-colored grids of various sizes. Buy paper with 1-inch lines clearly marked to enlarge patterns.

Masking tape: A tan or white removable adhesive paper tape.

Metal shears: Implement for cutting metal.

Mitered corners: Corners that are cut or folded to meet at an angle, usually 45 degrees on a right-angled corner.

Mod Podge sealer/glue: An adhesive especially made for gluing, sealing, and finishing decoupage.

Paper-backed fusible web: An iron-on adhesive for bonding one fabric shape to another. The paper backing allows you to cut the fabric and web as one piece before bonding.

Primer: A thin undercoat that seals the surface of wood before painting.

Removable tape: Any sticky-back tape, such as drafting, masking or clear-plastic tape, which is designed to temporarily hold in place and is easily removed.

Right side of fabric: The outer face you want showing on the finished project.

Roof flashing or sheet metal: Thin sheets of copper, tin, brass, or other metals sold in hardware, roofing, or crafts stores.

Round paintbrush: A round brush with bristles tapered to a point.

Seam allowance: The fabric between the stitching line and the cutting edge on sewn pieces.

Slip stitch: A blind stitch for sewing a folded edge to another folded edge, or for hemming more or less invisibly. Take a small stitch under the fold on one edge, then forward and under the fold or into the fabric of the other piece and repeat.

Smooth nap of velvet: The direction that feels smoother when you brush the nap in opposite directions with your hand.

Sponge painting: Dabbing paint on with a slightly damp natural or torn household sponge to create a mottled surface.

Stencil: A template cut for painting a repeated shape.

Stencil brush: An inexpensive round brush with stiff bristles and a flat tip for stippling paint through stencils.

Tacking stitch: A few small backstitches over each other or side by side to attach fabric or small decorations in place.

Tacky glue: A thick white glue that dries clear for adhering slightly bulky materials.

Template: A pattern cut from cardboard or other durable material for repeated use.

Tie wire: A flexible wire suitable for tying or wrapping one thing to another.

Topstitch: A line of straight stitching made on the outside of the fabric and intended to show.

Tracing paper: Paper you can see through for tracing. Use medium-weight paper for patterns.

Transfer paper: Paper, such as carbon paper, that will transfer marks from one sheet of paper to another paper or surface when under pressure.

White crafts glue: A common many-purpose, water-soluble white glue that dries clear.

Wire snips: Tool for cutting wire.

Wired chenille stem: Chenille yarn stiffened with wire, usually sold in 12-inch lengths; similar to a pipe cleaner.

Wrong side of fabric: The back of the fabric. On some woven fabrics, nylons or felt, the back is often hard to distinguish from the front. Choose the back and mark it.

Index to Projects

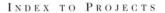

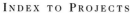

Uncle Sam Whirligig, 172

WREATHS

YARD ORNAMENTS

See Outdoor Decorations

CREDITS

CRAFTS DESIGNERS

Yvonne Beecher: 146 (ribbon roses); Joanne Beretta: 63, 86, 94, 96, 97, 151, 152, 156, 178; Stephanie Carter: 184; Rosemary Drysdale: 100; Nadia Hermos: 149; Margot Hotchkiss: 12, 188, 198; Richard Kollath: 41, 61, 71, 76, 78, 79, 82, 90, 105, 144 (dried flowers), 189, 211, 213; Kollath-McCann Creative Services: 7, 38, 47, 65, 66, 68, 72, 83, 195, 196, 205; Karin Lidbeck: 17, 18, 21; Cindy Lowrie: 58; Marsha Evans Moore: 159; Lina Morielli: 108; Ryl Norquist: 180; Cindy Taylor Oates: 3, 5, 176; Dolores Olson: 138, 140, 142, 144, 146, 148, 153; Brent Pallas: 35, 45, 74, 123, 175, 188, 208, 216; Jana Rosenfelt: 183; Joanna Randolf Rott: 106; Ginger Shafer: 99, 103, 141, 142, 143, 144 (reverse-print flowers); Mimi Shimmin: 36, 42, 48 (Pine-Woods Stocking), 52, 92, 115, 121, 124, 154, 164, 172, 200, 218; Robin Tarnoff: 9, 15, 23, 48 (Dangling-Stars, Little-Trees, and Snowfall stockings), 55, 57, 126, 128, 132, 135, 192, 202, 206, 214; Karen Taylor: 144 (appliqués); Jim Williams: 30, 32, 33, 118, 131, 170; Marianne Wourms: 27.

PHOTOGRAPHERS

Alban Christ: 120, 124, 132, 134, 152, 173, 176; Deborah Davis/Tony Stone Images: 1; Alistair Finlay: 117; Marco Franchina: 114, 118, 123, 143, 154, 157; Hunter Freedman: 40; Julie Gang: 180; Fred George/Tony Stone Images: 169; Kari Haavisto: 37, 89, 90, 92; Carol Havens: 113; Bill Holt: 34, 164; Len LaGrua: 26, 111, 138, 140, 141, 142, 144, 147, 148; Jill Levine: ii; Bruce McCandles: 139; Jeff McNamara: 2, 12, 17, 18, 19, 20, 23, 30, 32, 33, 41, 43, 48, 52, 55, 57, 65, 70, 75, 82, 83, 193, 195, 196, 198, 205, 206, 208, 210, 213; Tom McWilliam: 7, 14, 39, 45, 47, 62, 66, 68, 72, 126, 129, 131, 200, 203, 217; Keith Scott Morton, 185; Steve Mark Needham: 150; Luciana Pampalone: 86, 94, 96; Joe Polillio: 170, 179, 182, 191, 214; Lilo Raymond: 11, 108, 189; William Seitz: 58, 61, 77, 78, 79, 80, 102, 105, 106, 158; William Steele: 175, 188; Bruce Stoddard/FPG: 85; Marcus Tullis: 5, 99, 145, 153; John Uher: 149; Bernard Vidal: 9; Judith Watts: 100.